D1253418

WISDOM AT THE TOP
LESSONS ON LEADERSHIP AND LIFE FROM 35 CEOS

BY SCOTT D. ROSEN
PRESIDENT AND CEO, THE ROSEN GROUP AND TRANSFORMATIONS

authorHOUSE®

AuthorHouse™
1663 Liberty Drive
Bloomington, IN 47403
www.authorhouse.com
Phone: 1-800-839-8640

© 2010 Scott D. Rosen. All rights reserved.

No part of this book may be reproduced, stored in a retrieval system, or
transmitted by any means without the written permission of the author.

First published by AuthorHouse 6/15/2010

ISBN: 978-1-4520-3514-7 (e)
ISBN: 978-1-4520-3513-0 (sc)
ISBN: 978-1-4520-3512-3 (hc)

Library of Congress Control Number: 2010907967

Printed in the United States of America
Bloomington, Indiana

This book is printed on acid-free paper.

The CEOs in this book were interviewed by Scott Rosen in 2009 and 2010. Per
their recorded conversations, Scott Rosen indicated their interview profiles would
be compiled into a book for publication. The CEOs also provided permission to
be featured in the book by editing and approving their specific chapters.

Unless otherwise indicated, all photos included in this publication
are courtesy of the companies the CEOs work for.

Editorial assistance for this book was provided by Al Desetta, who offers
ghostwriting, developmental editing, and general book editing on a
wide range of topics. Visit his website: www.aldesetta.com.

This book is dedicated to my beautiful wife Risa, who has stood by me through thick and thin, and to my precious twin children Cassidy and Lee, who always remind me about what's really important in life.

CONTENTS

INTRODUCTION

BY SCOTT D. ROSEN,
PRESIDENT AND CEO,
THE ROSEN GROUP
AND TRANSFORMATIONS

The seeds for this book were planted early in my life.

I grew up in Trenton, N.J. and started my first real job when I was 12, working for Keith McKnight, who owned a chain of hoagie and pizza stores. Seeing an entrepreneur in action at a young age had a huge influence on me.

Keith was a very disciplined and hard-working guy. During the lunch blitz you might have 30 people waiting for hoagies. Keith would be slicing the cold cuts, I'd be adding the lettuce and tomatoes, and someone else was wrapping the sandwiches. We were a non-stop assembly line. All the while we'd be watching the customers, keeping track of how long they'd been waiting and what they wanted on their sandwiches. It was a simple but elegant lesson about the basics of running a business, one that I never forgot.

I went on to spend more than 20 years in corporate America, working for CIGNA, Prudential, and GE Capital. I spent half my corporate career in operations management, the other half in human resources. I learned a lot about managing people and leading teams. I had mentors who helped me identify my strengths and where to focus my talents. This experience was invaluable when I later started my own businesses.

Like many of the CEOs interviewed for this book, I felt the need to go out and run my own company. I felt restless in the corporate world. I was too much of a maverick to not strike out on my own. Maybe it was the entrepreneurial gene I inherited from dad.

My father was a very hard-working man. He owned a tavern and apartment buildings with his brother. Every day I saw my dad working his tail off to make his businesses thrive. I followed his example when I started my own company. During the first year or two, I was working 12 to 14 hour days to get it off the ground. I was constantly attending networking events, sales training programs, and classes. I consumed books about entrepreneurism, marketing, and sales. I was 110% committed, as an entrepreneur must be, to making my company successful.

That was 15 years ago. After much hard work, trial, and error, The Rosen Group, based in Voorhees, N.J., is a successful staffing company with revenue of $8.2 million in 2008. We specialize in placing human resources professionals, on both a temporary and permanent basis, throughout the New Jersey, Pennsylvania, and Delaware area. Some of our clients are GlaxoSmithKline, Philadelphia Coca-Cola, Comcast, Independence Blue Cross, and American Water.

After a number of years, I became restless again. I had been on a spiritual journey for many years, which included retreats, meditation, yoga, holistic health, and nutrition. I had never thought about making a business out of it, but decided to follow my passion. I hired someone to run my staffing company, did research, and studied similar programs around the country. In 2007, I founded Transformations, also located in Voorhees, which is now the Delaware Valley's premier holistic health and learning center. We feature speakers and workshops to help individuals, families, and communities realize their greatest potential.

After working in various businesses and starting my own, I had gained a great deal of respect for CEOs and corporate leaders. I understood the hard work and dedication that went into running a company. I understood the tremendous responsibility involved in creating quality products, serving satisfied customers, and retaining loyal and hardworking employees.

Therefore, I became troubled by the ways CEOs were depicted in the media during the great financial meltdown of 2008. Lehman Brothers, Bear Stearns, Merrill Lynch, AIG, and other companies either went under or were kept afloat by massive government bailouts, while, in too many cases, the executives who ran the companies into the ground walked away with huge compensation packages. The image of the privileged, greedy, and narcissistic CEO became firmly lodged in the public's mind. People were angry—and rightfully so—about the outrageous mismanagement of major companies that contributed to the economic disaster.

Yet, as I watched this image unfold in the media, I knew that it was just a very small and one-sided part of the story. The stereotype didn't apply to me or to the many CEOs I had known and worked alongside. I didn't come from a silver spoon background, but from a blue-collar one. My parents were not rich by any means. I wasn't handed jobs during my career. I came up through the ranks. I had to work my way up and earn them. The same was true for most of the CEOs I had met during my career.

Yes, there are some bad eggs out there. Yes, there is greed and narcissism and abuse in the corporate world. But most of the CEOs I've known are honest, down to earth, and caring people. They value their organizations and employees, and, far from being arrogant or reckless, they view themselves as stewards and protectors of important resources.

To set the record straight, I set out to interview CEOs in the greater Philadelphia area. Some of these men and women I had known for many years. Others were strangers before we sat down, talked, and became friends. They shared their time, experiences, and insights generously and openly, and I believe the lessons they have to offer transcend the business world.

I hope this book accomplishes three main goals.

First, I hope these stories challenge the media myth that CEOs are irresponsible, out of touch with the average person, and don't feel a sense of responsibility to their employees and communities.

Second, I hope you gain an understanding of the factors that make CEOs successful. I had many questions as I started my interviews. What were their upbringings like? Had they always wanted a career in business? Who influenced their career choices when they were growing up? How do they grow market share and maintain profitability? How do they gain loyalty from their customers, value their employees, and give back to their communities? How do they maintain balance and perspective, especially during difficult economic times? What leadership lessons do they have to impart? Their answers will surprise and enlighten you.

And finally, I want to pay homage to the CEOs and companies of the greater Philadelphia area—the hard-working, down-to-earth, salt of the earth environment where I was born and raised and have spent my working life. This book contains what I call "Rocky" stories—accounts of blue-collar people who came up through the ranks, worked their tails off, overcame challenges, and achieved success.

The lessons I've learned during my career are the same lessons revealed by the CEOs in this book—follow your passions, have the courage to take risks, and, whether you're sweeping the floor, making coffee at Starbucks, or running a million-dollar organization, do the best you can and good things will happen.

I wish you success in your career and hope you enjoy this book.

Scott D. Rosen
Voorhees, N.J.
March 1, 2010

ATTITUDE IS EVERYTHING

JOEL ADAMS, PRESIDENT, DEVON CONSULTING

Like many entrepreneurs, Joel Adams started his company in a rather modest setting—his second bedroom.

"I had an ironing board, a washing machine, and my desk," he told me.

Founding Devon Consulting back in 1982 was quite a risk for Adams, who never thought of himself as an entrepreneur. But success, in his view, is all about attitude.

"I thought, 'I'm not that kind of a risk taker,'" he said. "But entrepreneurs don't view risk in the same way as other people. For an entrepreneur, the risk is, 'I'll keep working for this company and my fate is in their hands. If I've got my own company, I have a lot more control over who's going to be laid off, and it won't be me.'"

Adams was working as a software salesman at the time, but was restless.

"I wanted to do something on my own," he recalled. "I wanted to be self-employed so I didn't have to put up with a sales manager I didn't like. That was my original goal, not to make $5 million or something like that."

Adams took the risk.

"Before I started the business, I was a commission salesman and had an incredible first four months of the year. I had the same amount of money in my checking account that I had earned the entire year before. So I had a cushion to get the business started. That's when I quit the software sales job."

Devon, located in Wayne, Pa., has since grown into a full scale staffing company, specializing in placing temporary, professional workers in the information services industry and in clinical trial administration. Revenue reached $11 million in 2008.

But, as with all chief executives, Adams has faced and overcome numerous challenges.

"If someone had laid out for me, step by step, all the difficulties and problems I'd encounter, I would have said, 'Oh my god, we can't do that.' But problems come up on a day-by-day basis, and that's how you deal with them. You solve today's problem today."

One of his first problems was cash flow. As every business owner knows, employees and bills need to be paid every week, but clients don't always pay their bills on a weekly basis. "You're profitable," Adams said, "but you don't always have the cash on hand to cover expenses."

To make up the shortfall, Adams used personal assets—stocks and bonds he had saved to buy a house—as collateral for bank loans during the company's early years.

"Eventually I found a house I liked, went to the bank, and said I needed my stocks and bonds back in exchange for the mortgage as collateral. The big bank said, 'What will we do for the three days between the time you cash the stocks and bonds and pay for the house? We'll have no collateral during that time. We can't do that.'"

Luckily, Adams found a local community bank that understood the needs of small businesses and was willing to immediately lend him $15,000 on his signature. "And they said when you need the other $10,000, come back and we'll put it on the mortgage." (That banker was Ted Peters, now Chairman and CEO of the Bryn Mawr Trust Company, also profiled in this book.)

But the greatest lesson Adams has to offer is not the nuts and bolts stuff, but attitude.

When asked for the advice he would give aspiring CEOs, Adams responded, "Confidence. You have to have the confidence that you will survive or succeed despite the obstacles thrown in your way."

Then, in his open, disarming way, Adams admitted that confidence has often escaped him as CEO. He said he learned to be optimistic only during the last three years, when Devon wasn't doing as well as in the past.

"The company was floundering, and either I didn't know why or wouldn't acknowledge why," Adams recalled. "I was afraid that I couldn't manage the sales process. I didn't have the confidence that I could make changes and they would come out all right. When the company started losing big sums of money, my optimism went out the window. I became very pessimistic and was having trouble sleeping."

Adams realized he had to work to change his attitude.

"I made a rule—I'm only watching comedies," he said with a smile. "No news, no dramas. Only reruns of *Seinfeld* and *Friends* because I couldn't take any more bad news.

"And then I picked up a Buddhist practice. Every day I would write down three things I appreciated and could give thanks for, instead of focusing on problems. I really came to the intellectual decision that it was my attitude that was holding us back."

At the time, Adams was talking to a business coach once a week.

"One day she said to me, 'Joel, I want to talk to you about one of my clients. He keeps talking about bankruptcy and saying he might have to sell his company.'

"I said, 'Sheila, I got it. I have to stop talking about that stuff and only about how we're going to be successful.'"

Adams wrote a phrase inside his pencil box, so he would see it every day: "Unfailing optimism and steadfast courage."

"That's what it takes," he told me. "And I'm so much happier than I was six months or a year ago. Devon has just as many problems as it's had many times in the past. I could be really upset and worrying about it. I could be unhappy, but I'm not. I'm very optimistic. The biggest change is not in the numbers but in my attitude."

Adams calls himself "an idea person" and derives enormous satisfaction from helping people start or improve their businesses. He has invested in half a dozen startup companies, either serving as an advisor to the founder or actually taking responsibility for sales and marketing for an initial period. He gave me a recent example.

"This 20-something kid calls me, a very nice person. He has an energy drink that he's designed and packaged. He doesn't have any money and is borrowing from his father. He wants someone to put up $750,000 so he can distribute it in every convenience store in six states. I told him I wasn't interested.

"Well, I thought about it all weekend. I called him back on Monday morning and said, 'You know what? You don't need my money—you need my advice. Can I be your mentor?' He says sure.

"So I flew down to Texas and met with him and all his people. They think they need $300,000 to run radio commercials, and they only have $40,000. And the kid is saying he wants to be the next big energy drink, doing $55 million a year.

"I got a big kick out of sitting around with them and talking about what markets they really wanted to be in. I said, 'Why would you want to be in a convenience store sitting next to the big energy drink that has a $50 million annual ad budget? Why not be where the competitor is not?' I helped them come up with a plan, focusing on what they would accomplish in the next 30 days. I got across a few things. His team left with a clear vision, as well as their short-term marching orders. He has since found someone to buy a chunk of the company and I hope he's successful."

But in the end, Adams pointed out, advice from other people can only go so far.

"Being a CEO is autodidactic," he said. "You have to learn on your own. Your company is going to be very different from everyone else's, even if you're in the same industry. What makes your company great is going to be personal to how you lead it, and that cannot be taught. You've got to be the CEO that you're comfortable being.

"CEOs will get plenty of conflicting advice all the time," he continued. "The best CEO is the one who is able to judge a situation and apply the right piece of advice to that situation. And I don't believe there is any way to teach that. You can read a lot of case studies. You can learn to see patterns of problems and ways to solve them. But which piece of learning you apply still comes down to the choices you make."

Finally, Adams emphasized that CEOs must never forget the example they set for their employees.

"In leading people, everything you do counts. It makes a difference if you show up wearing sneakers or shoes. It makes a difference if you smile and say good morning to your employees or have your head down. You may have your head down because your child got kicked off the Little League team, but your staff doesn't know that. If your head is down they immediately assume you're going out of business or that they're going to be fired.

"Everything you do affects the whole company and creates the culture of the company. What's most important to my employees are the little things I've said to them that I don't even remember. As a CEO you're always on stage, and you have to play the role every minute."

A FAMILY BUSINESS FLOURISHES

MARC BROWNSTEIN, PRESIDENT AND CEO, BROWNSTEIN GROUP

Many of the CEOs I interviewed never dreamed of a corporate or business career when they were kids. Not true in the case of Marc Brownstein. He was attracted to his father's advertising company from a very early age.

"I'm one of three kids," he told me. "I was the ad brat, the writer. When I was a kid, I was either playing hockey or writing. I loved coming into dad's office at an early age. He took me on client calls when I was three.

"He was really babysitting," Marc added with a smile, "but I always came into his office on school breaks. I wrote my first ad campaign at age 13 about a regional chain of sandwich shops."

Marc's father Berny founded what is now Brownstein Group back in March 1964.

"Dad was an artist, a fine painter," Marc said. "When his buddies were playing baseball, his passion was a paintbrush. He won a painting scholarship to the University of the Arts in Philadelphia. But then he realized, 'I got three kids, I better be making some money.'"

Brownstein's father turned his artistic interests in a new direction. He went to work for N.W. Ayer in Philadelphia, the country's first and biggest ad company. A few years later, with Marc's mother Beverly, he founded Brownstein Advertising.

Marc always planned to work in the business. After graduating from Penn State, where he cut his teeth running the school newspaper, he went to New York to learn best practices in the industry.

"I went from Happy Valley to Manhattan," he said, "and worked for Oglivy and Mather, the firm that was the smartest strategically and the best creatively. The plan was to work there two or three years, then go back and work in dad's firm.

"Well, after eight years in New York, my father asked me, 'Are you coming back?' I didn't think I would. I was starting to hit my stride. I was living in Manhattan. I had a wife and child, I was looking for homes. Dad is thinking, 'He's gone.'

"So finally he comes to New York and says, 'I really need you. I'm either going to bring you back or bring in a partner. Here's a plan I drew up. You'll do x, y, and z, and we won't step on each other's toes.'"

Marc's father wisely understood the challenges posed by family members working together.

"Dad did a lot of homework," Marc went on. "He spoke to other family businesses and patriarchs about how to do it right, so you have a functional family business rather than a dysfunctional one. Some family businesses need professional counselors in order to function. Fortunately, that's not the case with us."

Brownstein joked, "Partly that's because we limited family to just the two of us."

Marc came back to his father's firm in 1990 and the collaboration has been extremely successful in the years since.

"If we disagree, we have a lively debate and that's it. We share the same values. We want the same things for the business. We have never fundamentally disagreed and kept it there. We've always aligned our thinking."

Marc worked as creative director at Brownstein Group for seven years and was the strategic lead for the agency. Over time he evolved into CEO as his father gradually pulled away from the business (although Berny Brownstein is still very much involved in the firm).

Brownstein Group employs 65 people and earned $10 million in revenue in 2008. The company has offices in Philadelphia and Seattle, with clients primarily located in the Mid-Atlantic states and Pacific Northwest. Major clients include Microsoft, Comcast, Ikea, ESPN, and Goretex.

"We're a brand communication company," Marc told me. "We create unique brand identities for clients. But we're digitally centered as an agency, which means that we're non-traditional. Instead of thinking TV commercials, we're thinking, 'Where are the customers and how do we reach them?'"

That means going outside usual advertising venues.

"It might mean using Twitter," Marc continued. "For Ikea, we manage their global Facebook page. Our public relations team is managing blogs and writing on websites."

Brownstein said the company repositioned for the digital era about 10 years ago. They created a firm that built and marketed websites, which put them ahead of the curve in responding to the internet age.

Asked how he leads people, Marc stressed the importance of common ideals and goals.

"People may have different personalities," he said, "but what aligns them are shared values. We're clear about our core values. I want people who take smart risks. I want people who have sweaty palms in terms of their ideas, because their ideas scare them a little. I want people with fire in their bellies. I want people with integrity. I want wickedly smart people. I want people who think about 'we' rather than 'me.' The culture is very strong here and weeds out people who interview well, but who don't really share those values."

As CEO, Marc travels a lot and spends about 50% of his time on business development with new and current clients. Like many chief executives I interviewed, he's never complacent.

"I never feel secure. It's the nature of the business. As soon as I win an account, I worry about losing it. That just drives me to work harder to make sure we don't lose it. I have to touch that client on a weekly basis, which stretches you a bit."

Like many of the chief executives I spoke with, Brownstein benefits greatly from using other CEOs as mentors. He's the current chairman of the Young Presidents Organization (YPO), a group of dynamic CEOs from around the globe.

"I'm in awe of these guys. They learn about communication and productivity from me, and I learn how to manage in a more disciplined way. My graduate degree is from YPO."

Because of the pressures of their jobs, CEOs can face health risks. Brownstein finds balance from "two things—family and exercise."

"I'm still married to my bride," he said, "and I have three great kids. That gives me balance. And exercise—I belong to four gyms. In a creative business, it's essential. It wipes away stress, and keeps the blood flowing and the imagination firing. I also play golf, tennis, and take long bike rides."

For the future, Marc wants Brownstein Group to continue to lead the way by "staying on the cutting edge and always reinventing, even after 45 years."

"We embrace change, as long as it's in best interests of our clients and the agency. We come up with unexpected ideas and solutions for clients. We think like an Oglivy, but we behave like a nimble, two-person shop. A lot of companies come to us because they get frustrated with the cumbersome approach of large global networks that think about Wall Street and quarterly earnings, rather than the client's business."

How does he view his legacy?

"That I made a difference and did it the right way. My moral compass is very important to me. I sleep at night because I knew I did the right thing.

"I don't have a good memory, so I couldn't cover my tracks if I wanted to," he added, laughing. "That's what my dad taught me—do it the right way, so you don't have to look over your shoulder."

He encourages aspiring CEOs to "play to their strengths."

"It's a cliché but I really believe it: one, fill an unfilled need, something the marketplace needs, and two, make sure that need plays back to your strengths. If you do those two things, you'll find success. You can waste a lot of time doing too much or the things you're not good at."

Marc's last point is especially welcome, after recent corporate abuses.

"The greatest leaders aren't arrogant, but always believe they can improve and learn."

LITTLE THINGS MATTER

RICK A. LEPLEY, FORMER CEO, A.C. MOORE

As soon as we sat down to talk, Rick Lepley disclosed the personal touch he brings to his leadership role at A.C. Moore, the chain of more than 130 arts and crafts stores located throughout the eastern U.S.

"Here's an example," he said, "of the little things we like to do. There's an 83-year-old man who used to live in Florida. His wife died, so he moved back to Pennsylvania to be close to his children and grandchildren. His hobby is building dollhouses, and there was an article in the paper where he said he buys everything he uses at A.C. Moore.

"So I went to our customer relations person and said, 'You have to send this person a gift card.' And the man wrote back this wonderful letter that I just got today."

Rick was genuinely gratified as he reached across his desk to show me the note.

"It's often the little things that matter," he continued. "More so in this kind of business than in any other. This business is all about those kinds of people. You buy things in our store to fulfill some need for self expression. It's personal. You're not doing it to look good or to enhance an image."

Another aspect of the personal touch is the company's affiliation with Field Trip Factory, a program that takes kids and teachers on tours of stores to see how a retail operation actually works.

"We tie it in to our concept of 'Dream it, Create it, Share it.' When the tour of the store ends, they sit down and make something with our crafts before they leave. We do this year-round in all stores."

A.C. Moore also features a 10% discount program for teachers. The average teacher, Rick pointed out to me, spends $1300 out of his or her own pocket each year for materials that schools can't or won't supply.

Lepley joined A.C. Moore in 2006. He previously held high executive positions with Chrysler, Toyota, Mitsubishi, and Office Depot. Additionally, he managed several companies for his close friends, entrepreneurs Robert and Alan Potamkin of Philadelphia. Much of his career had been spent living and working in Eastern Europe and Japan, as well as throughout the U.S.

"Our family had literally gone around the world," Rick said. "Our kids were both born in South Jersey. Then we moved to California and eventually lived out of the country for eight years, including time in Poland, Hungary, and Japan. We lived in Florida for a time while I ran Office Depot's North American stores, and then we came back to work in the Philly area. It was like coming home after a very long road trip that lasted nearly 25 years. That felt good, since I was born, raised, and educated in Pennsylvania."

A.C. Moore, headquartered in Berlin, N.J., was founded in 1985 as a family-owned business. Its first store was established in Moorestown, N.J. The founder, Jack Parker, liked both Atlantic City and a character in a book named A.C. Moore. Thus the name.

"I wish he had called it something else," Rick said, breaking into one of the many hearty laughs that punctuated our talk, "because a lot of people come in here looking for house paint, mistaking us for Benjamin Moore."

While Rick believes it's critical that employees do their best, it's also important that people have fun coming to work.

"At the end of the day, it's not life and death. I tell my staff, 'Have fun, we're not selling nuclear waste here.' These are crafts. People should have a good time in our stores. If our employees are enjoying their work, our customers will enjoy the time they spend shopping with us."

Rick was brought in as CEO to completely rebuild the company's management team, and institute systems, procedures, and processes. A.C. Moore has been successful at achieving rapid growth, which Rick attributes to providing the widest selection of high quality merchandise at value prices. But when he first came on board, he said it took him a while to really understand the business and the level of challenges he faced. I asked Rick whether the challenges were part of the job's attraction.

"Absolutely," he said. "You're like a pennant contender always looking for a left-handed, 20-game winner. It took a while, but over time we have put together a good team."

Rick's new team rewrote the company's mission statement. They hired a consultant to identify common values in the organization and get people operating on the same page. Top management took personality tests to help them understand each other better and to work together more effectively. Project teams met to discuss goals.

"People know each other much better, and on a different, more personal level since we've done this," Rick told me.

I asked him if CEOs had a particular "DNA" in their genes. He wasn't so sure.

"Ulysses S. Grant said the things that impact you the most in life are the things you not only couldn't have planned, but that you didn't even know were happening at the time," Rick said. "Success might be as simple as being in the right place at the right time. In high school I envisioned myself becoming vice president of Chrysler Corporation. I had that vision, but I can't tell you exactly how life took me there. I love putting teams of people together to accomplish things."

Rick had that dream about Chrysler back in 9th grade when he was assigned a research project about his career goals. He wanted to become an executive at the automaker because of a man named Bob McCurry.

"My father was a Chrysler dealer and that's how I met Bob, who was executive vice president of North American operations. He was charismatic, a three-time All America football player at Michigan State. He was everything I wanted to be. And he was from a little town in central Pennsylvania very close to where I grew up. If he could do that, I wanted to do that too."

Eventually, Rick went to work for Chrysler, became Southern California regional manager in his 20s, and got to know McCurry. McCurry went to Toyota, asked Rick if he wanted to work there, and Lepley followed him. He still remembers that phone call as one of the most memorable conversations in his life. Rick eventually moved on to executive positions with Mitsubishi and Office Depot.

When I asked Rick for the advice he'd give to aspiring CEOs, he told me two stories.

"The first guy I worked for at Chrysler came back to the office one night and saw me still at my desk. I was probably 22 years old at the time. He was very impressed and said, 'Always remember it's what you do between 9 a.m.

and 5 p.m. that keeps you on the payroll, but what you do between 5 p.m. and 9 p.m. gets you promoted.' I never lost that thought.

"And my grandfather was in charge of transportation at a Baldwin Hamilton steel plant in my hometown and worked there nearly all his life. After he retired, as a little kid I'd sit on the front porch with him. When the shift changed at 3 p.m., the mill workers would be coming down the hill past our house. And I can remember understanding that they didn't like the new boss who had replaced my grandfather.

"One day the new boss came by and said he was having trouble managing the men. I remember this like it was yesterday and I don't think I was even eight years old. My grandfather said to him, 'I drove a mule team for John Miller when he owned the sand mine before World War I. And I learned that you get a better day's work out of the mule team if you drive them with a loose rein. You need to keep in mind that the same thing is true with men.'

"I don't get angry," Rick continued. "Our vice president of marketing made a mistake one day, and I was explaining to her why she made the mistake, and she said to me, 'I can't believe how calm you are.' And I said, 'What good would it do if I jumped on the table?' You can only get so far managing people with fear."

Like most company leaders, Rick worries about sales and making good decisions. There's also more on the plate if you're a public company (A.C. Moore is traded on NASDAQ).

"You want to do things perfectly, especially if you're a public company, and comply with all the rules," he said. "You want to do the right things, ethically and morally."

Rick told me he blows off steam through his hobbies.

"I love reading history, particularly the Civil War. I actually enrolled in a Civil War Master's program, but it took too much time and I never finished. When I was a little boy, my dad would take me to Gettysburg every summer. He'd show me my great-great-grandfather's name on the Pennsylvania statue. When I touched it, I had the sense that something important happened there and that my family was involved. Perhaps for a time I thought that my great-great-grandfather had single-handedly won the battle."

Rick continued, chuckling, "It took me a few years before I realized that every soldier from Pennsylvania who had been there in July 1863 had his name on the same statue."

I concluded by asking him about his vision for A.C. Moore's future.

"I hope it can become a national company," he said. "Part of the dilemma is how much cash we can use for growth without jeopardizing the company. That's the balance we're constantly trying to figure out, and the way the retail environment has been, we try to err on the side of being conservative.

"I'd like to leave a company that's still growing, that has a great foundation. I want it to be a place that operates with state of the art retail systems, with stores that customers find entertaining and full of creative ideas. And I want it to be a company where the employees look forward to coming to work every day. Some years ago, when I worked for Bruce Nelson, who at the time was Chairman and CEO of Office Depot, he used to tell me, 'We want to be a company that is a compelling place for people to shop, work, and invest.' I can't think of anything better than that. If we can do that, then maybe I'll move down to Gettysburg and open a little Civil War bookstore."

(Rick Lepley retired as CEO of A.C. Moore in March 2010.)

TRANSFORMING LIVES THROUGH ART

JANE GOLDEN HERIZA,
EXECUTIVE DIRECTOR,
THE CITY OF
PHILADELPHIA
MURAL ARTS PROGRAM

Photo by Shea Roggio for Philadelphia Magazine.

As a child, Jane Golden Heriza inherited a love of murals from her parents.

"They talked a lot about the artwork created in the Works Progress Administration (WPA) during the1930s," she told me. "My dad would bring home art books all the time and show me the work of Thomas Hart Benton, Ben Shawn, and Philip Guston. I grew up on those images. So I think I have this natural sense of appreciation for murals and what they mean to people."

That appreciation for public art has directed Jane's career path. She is now the Executive Director of the City of Philadelphia Mural Arts Program, one of the largest public arts programs in the U.S. Since 1984, the program has produced over 3,000 murals and educated over 20,000 underserved youth in neighborhoods throughout Philadelphia. Its success has attracted both national and international attention.

The program began in 1984 as a component of the city's Anti-Graffiti Network, an effort to eradicate graffiti in the city. As a muralist, Jane was to reach out to graffiti writers to redirect their energies to mural painting. Over the years, the program has provided a support structure for young people to develop their artistic skills, while they take an active role in beautifying their communities. The Anti-Graffiti Network was reorganized into the Mural Arts Program in 1996 with Jane as the director.

"We work with kids in prisons and shelters," Jane told me. "We don't discriminate about who gets opportunities in the arts."

The Mural Arts Program is a hybrid organization, what Jane calls "a really unique model for public/private partnership." Some 50% of the total budget comes from the city of Philadelphia, but 50% is raised privately. Of the 48 employees, 13 are city employees.

"I like to think of myself as a socially conscious entrepreneur," Jane went on, "so we have different potential sources of earned income. Students from the Fox School of Business at Temple University are helping us develop a strategic plan so we can market our consulting services to other cities. One source of income that's come to fruition is our Mural Tour Program, which has become hugely popular."

Jane told me the story of how she started with the organization. After graduating from Stanford University she moved to Los Angeles, where she painted murals and worked with kids on probation. She then became very ill with lupus and moved back east to be with her family.

"As I started to get healthier, I read an article in which Wilson Goode, the first African-American mayor of Philadelphia, described a new program that was dedicated to helping kids who were writing on walls. I felt this was an interesting mix of my interests in government, art, sociology, education, and the inner city. I love murals because of what they mean in the life of the city. So I applied and was hired to work part-time in the Anti-Graffiti Network."

Jane started meeting with kids who were graffiti writers and talking to community members. She went back to her boss and asked if she could do mural projects, and he was open to the idea.

"He took me to the Spring Garden Street Bridge in West Philadelphia. It's 600 feet long and made of corrugated metal. Oh, it was awful. There was graffiti everywhere. This was 1985, when there was a graffiti crisis in Philadelphia. So he challenged me. He said, 'If you can work with a group of kids from this neighborhood and put up murals here in three weeks, I'll consider you for a full time job.' So I worked with an extraordinary group of young people, we met the deadline, and they hired me."

From 1985 to 1990, Jane helped grow the art component within this anti-graffiti program.

"I felt it was my responsibility to try to mine young people's artistic potential and put them to work in productive ways. They had been drawing from comic books since they were young. They had an intuitive sense of design and color and anatomy. I wanted them to look at the path they were on—not just graffiti, but selling drugs, taking drugs, and minor theft. This was going to lead them to Graterford Prison. It was very important to shine a light on their lives in a way that wasn't punitive, and let them know that they had other options because of their talents. The Anti-Graffiti Network ended up being an incredible vehicle for kids to change their lives."

Since graffiti is done surreptitiously at night, I wondered how Jane was able to round up the kids.

"I had about a dozen community organizers working with me. We had huge maps in our office, we knew where the graffiti writers hung out, where the graffiti gangs were, and we would go to them.

"I can't tell you how many times I would go to recreation centers, to drug corners, and start talking to kids about joining our program. We were pretty fearless when I think about it, because Philadelphia had poverty in capital letters during the mid to late 1980s. We were going into neighborhoods where the only city workers were the police, period. But it was incredibly rewarding, because we were always able to come away with a couple of kids signed up. Once they signed up, I had faith that they would somehow change.

"The big draw was jobs. First they had to sign a pledge that they'd never write on walls for the rest of their lives. We knew that wasn't true, but once they did some scrub time cleaning graffiti they were eligible for employment as mural artists. So it was really about paying jobs, and I had a very big carrot in my hand. If I was just offering an arts program for four weeks, it wouldn't have been appealing at all."

The program ran workshops at churches, community centers, and the Philadelphia Museum of Art. It just took off. By the late 1980s and early 1990s, the Anti-Graffiti Network had summer programs with thousands of kids working and painting murals. It was then reorganized as the Mural Arts Program in 1996.

I asked Jane how her illness has affected her career.

"Having lupus is a mixed blessing," she said. "You realize your mortality, and you have to figure out how to make peace with the illness because it's not going away. It's an autoimmune disease and there's no cure. It's a little bit like cancer—it goes in and out of remission.

"When I was diagnosed in 1982 I was quite ill and told I wouldn't live long. So that was devastating and I had to figure out how to deal with it. Then there are times when I'm in great pain and sometimes it manifests itself with low-grade fevers. I haven't had a flare up in a few years, but it can be unpredictable. I could get a cold, and in two weeks end up in the hospital with pleurisy.

"And so you try to make every minute count. It's given me a sense of perspective and, interestingly enough, helped me relate to the kids I worked with in Anti-Graffiti. We were from two different worlds and our common ground was our mutual love of art. But I also think I related to them because, in a sense, I too was an outsider."

What stood out in my interview with Jane was her belief in the power of art to transform lives.

"I think one of the hardest things in life is for us to see things from another point of view. When that happens, when your perception has shifted, even slightly, I find that to be a victory, a triumph of the human spirit, in a sense, and that's what I love about the work.

"Tomorrow, I'm speaking to a group of 25 kids who participated in our program. A few years ago, they were in and out of the juvenile court system. Today, at least half of them are either attending community college or are enrolled at the Art Institute of Philadelphia. This is a huge victory, and even sweeter when you understand the obstacles that they had to overcome.

"We haven't always succeeded. We've lost some kids. We've had a few kids die, and there's a fellow in one of our classes at Graterford Prison serving life without parole. He's an enormously talented artist, and every time I see him I ask myself, 'How did we let him get away? What did we do wrong? What could we have done better?'"

THE CLIENT COMES FIRST

TED PETERS,
CHAIRMAN AND CEO,
BRYN MAWR TRUST
COMPANY

Unlike most bank presidents, Ted Peters isn't hidden away from public view in an upstairs corner suite. Instead, his office is just off the main floor of the Bryn Mawr Trust Company, with full access to any client. This is more than a symbolic gesture on the part of Peters. Openness, access, and client satisfaction characterize his fundamental approach to the banking business.

"I could easily be upstairs," Peters told me. "But we're still a regional community bank, and lots of people stop by and say hello all the time. I want to be visible and accessible."

Local business people founded the Bryn Mawr Trust Company in 1889. In 1955 the company merged with the Bryn Mawr National Bank. For years the firm has connoted longevity, strength, and security in the Philadelphia area.

Peters became CEO of Bryn Mawr Trust in 2001. The company's long-time chief executive was retiring, and Peters, who had previously started and then sold a couple of banks, was contacted about his interest. He threw his hat into the ring, although at the time, he said, "I joked that the only thing I knew about 'trust' was that it had five letters."

Perhaps so, but during his last eight years at the helm Peters has grown the bank impressively. Assets were $400 million when he came on board;

they now total $1.2 billion. In the 16 years before he became CEO, Bryn Mawr Trust hadn't built a single new branch. They've opened four in the last six years.

"We've accomplished a lot," Peters said, "but at the same time, we want to make sure we maintain the quality of the brand.

"We don't have customers," he continued, "we have clients. We're not selling money, we're selling relationships. We've always had a great sense of caring for the community and for the clients. We're known for obsessive service."

When Bryn Mawr Trust recently conducted surveys of client satisfaction, the firm conducting the surveys thought the data was wrong. "They had never seen scores that high," Peters said. "Some 99% of clients were happy with the bank."

Bryn Mawr Trust promotes not just a culture of client service, but also of employee satisfaction. "We have a tremendous community here," Peters noted. "Employee dinners, picnics, softball teams, holiday parties. The Bank is like a family to our employees. It's important to treat people fairly, pay them fairly, and give them job security."

Bryn Mawr Trust has two main businesses. It's a community bank with nine full-service branches. The community bank includes a mortgage and insurance company. It also runs a trust company, which helps people manage assets and trusts, and companies set up 401K and pension plans. The company is well known for it's fiduciary trust, which manages trusts, wills, and estates. The wealth management part of Bryn Mawr Trust oversees some $2.3 billion in assets.

A publicly traded company listed on NASDAQ, Bryn Mawr Trust also has a large business with local non-profit organizations. Its non-profit practice includes private schools, colleges and universities, churches, synagogues, social service agencies, clubs, museums, and civic and fraternal organizations.

Did Peters dream of becoming a bank CEO as a kid?

"Not at all," he replied. "I thought I was going to be a college lacrosse coach."

Peters calls himself "a typical Philadelphian. I've never lived more than five miles from where I was born, which was Bryn Mawr Hospital, except for Amherst College in New England for four years."

After attending the Haverford School and graduating from Amherst in 1972, Peters taught school for four years. Then, in his mid-twenties, he joined the commercial lending training program at Philadelphia National

Bank and over four years worked his way up. In 1984, bitten by the entrepreneurial bug, he and some of his clients got together and decided to start their own bank.

"I look back and think that we must have been crazy," Peters said. "We had no idea what we were doing. I was 34, already had three kids, and my wife was pregnant. I had a very good job at IVB as a regional vice president. It couldn't have been a nicer place to work, but we just had this idea about starting something up."

Peters took the risk. He left the bank, set up an office in his basement, raised capital, got a charter, and found a site in Wayne for the National Bank of the Main Line. They did very well. "For years, we were the most profitable new bank east of the Mississippi."

After seven years, Peters and his partners sold the bank to a holding company in Harrisburg. Peters worked for the company, but he was used to calling his own shots. Once again, he caught the entrepreneurial bug. "This time I was really crazy," he recalled, "because I was doing very well."

Peters left the holding company and started the First Main Line Bank above a hoagie shop in Paoli. He and his corporate partner opened branches, built assets, and grew the bank to over $200 million in assets. It was merged into a holding company upon his departure to Bryn Mawr Trust.

Peters, who was just elected to the board of the Philadelphia Federal Reserve in January, 2010, has this advice for aspiring CEOs.

"Sometimes it can be lonely at the top. Surround yourself with people who will tell you exactly what they think. I have a CFO who's a brilliant guy, we're good friends, and yet we go at it all the time. You have to be open and willing to accept criticism and admit mistakes. If you screw up, tell people. I've screwed up plenty of times.

"And to be a successful entrepreneur," he added, "you have to be a self-starter. I'm out two or three nights a week talking to groups and meeting new people. I have lunch and breakfast every day with people I've never met before and love it."

Peters said it's also important to keep your work in perspective and not take it too seriously. "I remind myself that there's a billion Chinese who haven't heard of the Bryn Mawr Trust Company. We're in a serious business, but it's also important to enjoy what you're doing."

Earlier in his career, Peters did all the detail work. His typical day now is the big picture: "Where do we expand and how do we do it? Do we start a new company? Do we make an acquisition? I leave the details to others.

There's nothing better than growing and winning deals and building the business.

"My job is to turn it over to the next person in better shape than when I got it. I've taken something good and hopefully have made it stronger, bigger, and more profitable. Being CEO is really a form of stewardship. I want to walk away and say, 'I'm proud of what I did.'"

Peters believes the recent abuses by CEOs are in the bigger public companies and are committed by perhaps 1% of chief executives.

"I've never seen such egregious abuses before, but they're committed by a small number of CEOs. The American people get upset, and rightfully so, when someone runs a company into the ground and then walks away with a huge compensation package. The problem lies not only with the CEOs, but also with boards and compensation committees that are not paying attention and doing their duty to the shareholders.

"We should go to the Japanese or British model," Peters continued, "and set a limit on CEO compensation. In big companies we have crazy numbers. CEOs were traditionally paid 20 or 30 times the average compensation of employees, but in some companies that's moved up to 300 or 500 times the average pay."

While Peters has always worked very hard throughout his career, he's never sacrificed his family or personal life.

"I had four daughters who were active in sports," he noted. "I made all their games, but then I'd go back to the office at 7 p.m. and put in a couple of more hours. I think I saw 44 field hockey games in one year. That has to be some kind of a record."

THE CALCULATED RISK

HAROLD T. EPPS, PRESIDENT AND CEO, PRWT SERVICES INC.

As President and CEO of PRWT Services Inc., Harold T. Epps leads an extremely diversified workforce and one of the largest minority-owned firms in the country. For nine consecutive years, it has been named one of Black Enterprise's Top 100 Companies in America.

"We try to be a model of diversity," Epps told me. "Our employees are 50% male, 50% female. In terms of race, 50% are what America calls minorities, 50% majority. We have both rural and urban locations for our facilities. We are a very diverse company in terms of our products, services, population, and geography."

A privately held company based in Philadelphia and employing about 1,500 people, PRWT offers a wide range of business process solutions, large-scale facilities management, and pharmaceutical manufacturing and value added services.

"Business Process Solution is the name for our outsourcing company," Harold explained. "We manage the parking ticket systems for Philadelphia, Los Angeles, California, and San Francisco. We manage the E-Z Pass system for the states of New Jersey and New York. We've been in that business for 22 years.

"We also currently manage over 20 million square feet of space spread across the United States," Epps said. "For example, the Thurgood Marshall Federal Judiciary Building, which houses offices for the Supreme Court, and Philadelphia's TRI-PLEX of municipal buildings."

Epps was born in Winston-Salem, North Carolina. His family moved to Asheville, N.C., but then back to Winston-Salem when his father died of pneumonia when Epps was 12.

That's where Epps finished junior and senior high school. He then earned an undergraduate business degree from a historically black university, North Carolina Central University.

Immediately after college Epps went to work for the Digital Equipment Corporation (DEC), where he spent 19 years, becoming the youngest plant manager in the company's history. While working at DEC, he also earned an M.B.A. from Western New England College.

"I had sixteen fabulous years," Epps told me, "two so-so years, and one pretty miserable year, which was the last year. DEC was downsizing and closing plants, and during December of that year I was in negotiations about when my plant was going to have to close.

"Through some tenacious work, I got wind that the severance package offered to employees was going to change on January 1, 1993, from three weeks pay for every year of service, to two weeks. I decided I was going to get the best deal I could for my employees. I wasn't going to sit by and let 10, 15, or 20 weeks of pay be taken from the pockets of hard-working people who owned houses and had kids in college. Not for some arbitrary, artificial reason.

"So I declared on December 21, 1992 that the plant would be closing to ensure the employees would be offered the original severance package and avoid the January 1, 1993 change. I told them it would close sometime between April and December 1993. I wanted the employees to know what was happening before they went out and spent all that severance money. When I saved the original package for them, they gave me a standing ovation."

After leaving DEC, Epps became the general manager of a subsidiary of Polaroid that trained economically disadvantaged individuals in job skills, so they could then find entry into the mainstream workforce with other companies. After two years there, and 20 years altogether in manufacturing, Harold decided he wanted to run a company.

"I set that as a goal for myself," he said. "I concluded that I needed some sales and marketing experience to reach my goal. I could not find that opportunity in Boston because I'd been labeled a manufacturing guy."

Then, to explain the risks he had taken in his career, Epps shifted to telling me about his childhood experiences in the civil rights battles in the south.

"When I was in the fifth grade in Ashville, North Carolina, in 1962, I integrated a school system. I was the first black to go to school there. I had gone to segregated schools, and my father, a lawyer, finally said no to that. He was prepared for a big legal fight, and the principal said, 'Okay, it's about time, come on.'

"So we got slapped around a little bit and spit on, but no water hoses, none of that stuff that went on in Alabama and Mississippi. I'm telling you this story because now I'm out looking for a sales and marketing position, and a company in Neenah, Wisconsin, about 100 miles north of Milwaukee, said they had something called 'a general manager in waiting' program. They wanted to hire about six to eight rising leaders, bring them to their corporate headquarters, have them learn the company, and then place them in openings within a year. In my case they had never had an African-American executive before and they wanted that. So I said, 'I'll make a deal with you. I don't have any sales or marketing experience, but I'm pretty smart. I'll come and be your trailblazer, if you give me the chance.'

"People thought I had absolutely lost my mind to take a job in what seemed like the middle of nowhere, but if I had not taken what I call controlled or calculated risks, I would not be sitting here talking to you today. As a result of that first step, I acquired the skills and the knowledge to run mid-sized companies.

"I subsequently ran three different mid-sized companies, between $50 million and $200 million in size. They were all in transformation, either undergoing a growth spurt or needing to be turned around and reorganized.

"I did that in Milwaukee for three years," Harold told me. "I ended up being rated the number one general manager in the company. Then they wanted me to move to Fort Wayne, Indiana, to take on a bigger task. I'm saying, 'Oh no, I can't go to Fort Wayne. Too small, just too conservative.'

"They came back and said becoming president is in your future. You can write your own ticket, we need you to go. Well, you can say no only so many times. So I started out with an $80 million unit and in two years was promoted to running a $100 million unit. Subsequently I became president of North American operations for the combined unit, and in about four years took it from breakeven to 12% EBITDA, and then we sold it."

Epps joined PRWT as president in November, 2007 and became CEO in October, 2008.

I asked whether he always saw himself as a leader.

"In fifth grade, my two sisters and I were the first African-Americans to enter in that school. By the next year I was president of the student body. When we moved back to Winston-Salem, I became president of the student body in the ninth grade and I was president of my sophomore class, my junior class, and my senior class in high school.

"I always gravitated toward leadership. I was always the first to organize the softball, baseball, and basketball games in the park. I think it starts with the ability to listen and not prejudge. At the same time, I do not allow individual agendas to supersede the core mission. The institution is more important than any individual. I have not been afraid to affirm that if pushed that far. I'll play baseball with them. Strike one, strike two, and strike three, you're out. I've had to do that on plenty of occasions, because if you don't, you lose the respect of the organization."

When I asked Epps to describe his greatest influences, he put as much emphasis on community as on family.

"With me, it starts with family members. Although I had my father for only 12 years, it starts with him, and a very strong mother. I needed a male figure to help me get through the teen years, and my grandfather was an excellent, stabilizing force. In the neighborhood I lived in, which was segregated, everybody was your mentor, from the preacher, to the teacher, to the mailman. You might cut grass for this one, watch baseball with that one, or go to the ballgame with another one. Everybody was involved in raising you. The saying that it takes a village to raise a child—that was the culture that I was raised in."

I asked Epps whether that was a culture of the south or of race.

"Neither. I think it was our society's culture when we were less mobile, knew our neighbors, and families were more intact. When I grew up you could leave your door open. You sat on your porch and talked with people. Now, about 50% of marriages end in divorce. We have all these kids in one-parent households. All of that just leads to an entirely different kind of support system."

That sense of connection, so often lacking in our communities, is fundamental to good business, Epps told me.

"The final guiding principle I'll mention would be this: practice the 'R' before the 'I'. In other words, put the relationship before the issues. If I'm going to do a sales call or if I see you as a prospect, I'm going to invite you to play golf or take you to a baseball game, and I'm not likely to talk business at all. Before we get to that, we're just going to get to know each other."

RESPECTING THE EMPLOYEE

DAVE GRIFFITH, PRESIDENT AND CEO, MODERN GROUP LTD.

Deep caring and respect for his employees permeated my conversation with Dave Griffith, President and CEO of the Modern Group.

Founded 64 years ago by Dave's father-in-law, the Modern Group sells, repairs, and rents industrial equipment, such as forklifts, aerial work platforms, generators, light towers, and construction equipment. It is one of the largest privately-held rental companies and material handlers in the U.S. Located predominantly in the mid-Atlantic states, Modern currently employs about 540 people in some 22 locations.

"Not a terribly sexy industry," Griffith told me in his down to earth manner. "Nobody grows up and says I want to be in forklifts or in cranes. But it's a pretty solid business. People are always going to need to store stuff, build stuff, and move stuff."

What sets Modern apart from most companies is that it has been 100% employee owned since 2003. The company features an Employee Stock Ownership Program (ESOP), which was started in 1984. Employees are in the program after 1,000 hours of service, vest in the program after three years, and are granted shares once a year based on company performance. Everyone gets the same percent of salary as a contribution.

"Our stated goal is to be a great company by being a great ESOP company," Griffith said. "I believe passionately in employee ownership.

"Everything we make stays in the business," he added, noting that the company has a target of 8% of compensation going into the ESOP program. "In 63 years of business, 52% of the retained earnings have flowed to the employees, either in terms of an ESOP contribution, a 401k match, a dividend, or an outright cash bonus. The company stock has averaged a 10.4% annual increase."

Since an ESOP is tax deferred, there are substantial tax benefits for employee ownership companies. Modern used to have a 44% tax rate; it is now 8%. But Griffith is most proud of how ESOP has affected employee morale, productivity, and loyalty.

"As an ESOP, our employees understand that they're owners," Griffith said. "Remember that 52% number—for every dollar they save, half of that essentially goes to them." This understanding, he noted, creates a different attitude in the workplace.

"An employee might be willing to say, 'Look, I know I'm a mechanic, but tell me what you need me to do. I can drive today, or I can put parts away, or I can come in Saturday and paint the branch.' I have branches where the guys come in on Saturday to fix the van rather than send it to the shop.

"As we interview people to come here, they will tell you that this is a different place to work. We were voted one of the best places to work by the Pennsylvania Chamber of Commerce. We were runner up in the Ernest and Young Entrepreneur of the Year Program for our ESOP program."

Griffith started his career as an engineer for IBM in New York City in 1976. He held a variety of positions with the company, advancing up to regional manager. He then worked for Siemens, before moving on to run marketing for national accounts at MCI.

"By that time we had moved 14 times and loved it, but my wife and I had two small kids." In September, 1992, Griffith decided to go to work for the company his father-in-law had founded in 1946.

He didn't start out as CEO. "My father-in-law brought me in as vice president of marketing for six months. I went around and learned the business. I ran one division, then two divisions. Then after about four years I became president. We started to do acquisitions, and the company evolved from a family-run small business into a larger entity. It wasn't always smooth, but we worked it out. I bought into the business and stretched, just like every owner.

"We built structure and process into the business. We built marketing, tech, and HR functions. Modern had always been a good, professional company, but where my father-in-law could go out and literally make every decision, we now hired and trained people so I could focus on strategy, infrastructure, and the things necessary to run a business."

As another indication of his respect for his workers, Griffith has employed an open door/open book management style as CEO, an approach he learned and valued at IBM.

"Open book says we share all the numbers," Griffith said. "When I ran a branch at IBM, I shared all the numbers with them. It's important that employees know what the challenges are and that you're shooting straight with them. You tell the truth and don't sugarcoat it. You never want to underestimate people's ability to understand reality."

Every month, Griffith circulates a memo on company performance— "the good, the bad and the ugly," as he put it—and the memo that goes to Modern's board is identical to the one that goes out to all employees. This open approach, Griffith said, has served the company incredibly well, especially in bad times.

"We had an off-cycle where we did salary cuts and layoffs. And in the memos we said here's what we're doing, the leadership team is taking a pay cut, we're freezing salaries, we looking at layoffs, we're closing a branch, etc. But the other side of that is telling your employees specific things they can do to help. And then you try and have the organization reinforce that."

In addition to running an open book on financial performance, Griffith employs an open door policy to build a company culture where good ideas flow and conflicts are resolved quickly.

"Any Modern Group employee has the right to go anywhere in the organization and talk to any employee, without fear of retribution. And we have company roundtables. My CFO and I go out and meet with employees and ask them what they want to talk about. I want a culture where we don't let problems fester, where employees are able to ask questions and get straight answers. I don't know another way to manage."

Griffith's day-to-day management style is hands-on. He leaves two hours open every day to visit departments and call employees. He tries to contact every branch manager at least once a month, to get a feel for how things are going.

"My mantra is, 'Wear muddy boots.' That comes from my dad. You can't manage from behind a desk."

What keeps Griffith up at night?

"Fundamental demand and the consequences if there's no demand. How do I protect jobs? How do I protect benefits? I spend a lot of time thinking about strategy. What are the moves we should be making?"

About nine years ago, Modern's business mix was about 55% sales, with the balance parts, service, and revenue. Looking at sales margins in its various businesses, the company made a conscious decision to go after and grow the service sales capability. They changed the focus of the rental fleet and, for diversification reasons, made sure that no one vender constituted more than 20% of revenue. They accomplished this strategy over a couple of years. New equipment sales now represent 40% of business.

"About 40% of what we service we didn't sell, but we're doing the service on it—repairing, fixing it, putting parts in it," Griffith said. "At the end of the day, we're a service house and a rental house."

Looking to the future, Griffith believes Modern can be substantially bigger and more profitable. He wants to grow the business selectively, finding additional products that fit the existing portfolio.

What would he say to aspiring CEOs?

"I'd give the same advice dad gave. Be curious and never accept current results. Dad had a great expression, 'When you're coasting, you're going downhill.' There's a lot of wisdom in that. You've got to be insanely curious. If you accept today's numbers, relax, and go on cruise control, you'll die in moments."

He went on: "A lot of innovation we've done here is because we went to a trade show or took a class or we sent someone off to a school, and they found something interesting. The challenge is to look at a technology or a process, and extrapolate from that what you can use. A great example of that in this business is GPS. We adopted it very early on and use it for dispatch or to find technicians without calling them. That helps us be efficient and get ahead of the curve."

When Griffith's father died, he left a substantial estate. Dave and his brother used that money and added their own to start the Griffith Family Foundation, a project he feels very strongly about. The foundation concentrates on financial assistance for students in need.

When Griffith discusses the legacy he'd like to leave behind, he brings it back once again to his employees.

"This will sound like a cliché, but it's never about me. My job is real simple: to make sure we do a great job of hiring and then get those people what they need to succeed. That's the definition of being a good CEO. I don't have a big ego to feed. If I can leave behind a great company that preserved and grew jobs, that's just fine."

STAY ON GOAL

MARK BAIADA,
PRESIDENT AND
FOUNDER,
BAYADA NURSES

"Our mission is to make it possible for millions for people worldwide to experience a better quality of life with comfort and dignity," Mark told me.

Bayada Nurses, the company Mark founded in 1975 with his hard-earned savings, provides nursing, rehabilitative, therapeutic, and personal home health care services to children, adults, and seniors in their own homes. Headquartered in Moorestown, N.J., the company has over 12,000 health care professionals working from more than 170 offices in 18 states. Bayada Nurses was on target to earn over $600 million in revenue in 2010.

The story behind the company's success, like so many in this book, is fascinating.

Mark grew up in South Jersey and from early on knew he wanted to someday own a business.

"I had two different paper routes," he said. "Every time it snowed I would run and shovel for someone. And the Italians have businesses. My grandfather had a barbershop. My uncle had a warehouse. So I kind of knew I was going to have one."

Mark attended Rutgers University, first in Camden, then in New Brunswick, and earned an MBA. After graduation, he set goals for himself.

"I took charge of my life. Most people go down the river of life on an inner tube. Wherever it takes them, they kind of deal with it. I said no, I'm going to pick a goal and head there, and I'll have a better chance than if I just float down the river.

"My goal was to have a business, but I had a couple of deficits. The first was no money. I had debt from college. The second was that I was insecure about my business abilities because I figured, 'Oh my God, my mother was an immigrant, my father was the son of two Italian immigrants. What do I know? I have an education, but the people who run big businesses know everything.'

"So I had to learn about business and save my money. I wouldn't spend. I wouldn't go to McDonald's. I drove a Volkswagen. I wouldn't buy a winter coat. I was so cheap, but it didn't bother me. I figured I'd get in business faster."

Mark began his career doing marketing research for companies. He enjoyed the problem-solving aspect of the field.

"A lot of people try to solve a problem with available information, rather than what information is necessary to solve the problem. I like to see a problem and then get the proper information to solve it.

"In the meantime, I wanted to become a student of American business. I set out to learn as much as I could. I had stacks of annual reports. I would think about what made a particular business a success or a failure."

To gain experience, Mark explored every avenue.

"Somebody asked me to take over a defunct Cub Scout pack and I figured that would give me managerial experience. So at 23, I was running a Cub Scout pack."

At the time, Mark was living in Bridgeport, Conn., and working for a company called American Thread. He had an apartment for $75 a month and was saving money every way he could.

"Then I got a call from a headhunter. He asked me if I wanted to work for a company that the Harvard Business Review had called the best-managed company in America. I said that's right up my alley.

"So I went to work for Avon in Manhattan. I stayed there for a few years, and went from the manager of marketing, planning, and research to a research associate. I was still in saving mode. I had an inexpensive New York apartment, a sixth floor walkup, $235 a month. Mr. Englebert was the landlord. He was in his 80s, and every time I would go pay my rent we'd talk business. He bought and sold properties all around the upper west side, and he taught me a lot early on.

"By now I had a certain confidence. It was the spring of 1973. I'd worked for two major companies. I had talked to a lot of people. So I said, I think I'm ready to find a business.

"How was I going to do that? Being in marketing and research, I knew I had to have criteria. First, I had saved $16,000 to work with. Two, I wanted to feel good about what I was providing, that the business had a social benefit. I wouldn't put up a casino or go into alcohol or cigarettes. I wanted to feel good about making the world a better place. And third, I wanted to go into a growing field, where the demand for the service was steadily increasing on a long-term basis. Find something that's needed and that's going to grow, grow, grow.

"So there were a lot of things I looked at. Early childhood education was one, because it was growing, but I wasn't trained in early childhood education. I didn't feel competent that I could take care of kids during the most formative times of their lives.

"Then I saw an ad in *The New York Times* for a business for sale. Quality Care, a franchise taking care of the elderly. I go, 'Whoa.'

"I knew the demographics were good. So all of a sudden it kind of clicked and I went to talk to them and everything fell into place fairly quickly. I went to the library again. I found out that the number of elderly is increasing steadily and is extremely predictable. Mortality tables and rates are very stable. The number of elderly was going up then and it's still going up. Who was going to take care of them?

"The next social factor was the breakdown of the extended family. My grandmother lived with me, my mother lived with me when she had a stroke, but that's unusual now. You don't have three and four generation households.

"So I thought, the elderly are out there looking for somebody to take care of them. I'm going to do it."

Manhattan was too big an area, and South Jersey was too small, not developed like it is now, so Mark chose Philadelphia. He rented a small office on Walnut Street for $125 a month.

"When I started out, I did everything myself," he told me. "I designed all the forms, designed the logo, I incorporated myself. I started advertising, and gradually the business picked up. We had cases.

"All of a sudden, one of my home care workers doesn't go to work. Well, what's this all about? My adrenalin kicks in. I want the business to be perfect. I realize I have a crisis.

"A couple of Bayada Way principles set in right then. One, when the clients call, tune into their problem, take responsibility for the solution, and help them solve it. So if there was a problem, I would fix it fast."

Mark said the company's core values are compassion, excellence, and reliability.

"The problem in this business isn't the employee's ability to do the work, it's the ability to show up day in and day out. Reliability is the key thing. No matter what it takes, just be there and do what you say you're going to do. Never let anybody down. There's an art to this ability to trust in relationships. So I treat people with respect, tune in to the client's needs, and keep my commitments."

At a certain point, Mark realized that being a perfectionist was not a good value for a leader.

"Whenever there was a problem, I felt I was letting people down who were counting on me. Sometimes I thought maybe I should quit, because I wanted the business to be perfect and I couldn't be perfect. I was driving myself crazy about making everything just right.

"Then one day the answer came to me. Guess what, Mark? You don't have to be perfect, because perfect doesn't exist. If a client goes to another agency, that agency isn't going to be perfect either. All I can do is continue to try to be the best."

In his extensive reading and research on what makes companies and people successful, Mark boils it down to one key principle—making the right choice in the present moment.

"People who become successful set a goal and stay on the goal, which means they're fully, totally engaged. They're in the flow. In each moment, they're on their goal. It's like being an athlete in the middle of a sports event—you'd better be alert to what's happening and what you need to do. This applies to business or anything else you do—in each moment, just stay on goal."

KEEPING AN EYE ON THE BIG PICTURE

RICHARD P. MILLER, PRESIDENT AND CEO, VIRTUA

When Richard Miller was a kid, he wasn't focused on a career in business. He grew up in a working class family in a row house in South Philadelphia, and thought he would one day play third base for the Phillies. Yet the experiences of his youth have had a major influence on his leadership role at Virtua, the largest health services provider in South Jersey.

"My mom and dad worked in a factory—Baker Clothes, on 26th and Reade, down in South Philadelphia," Rich told me. "That's where they met. My dad was modeling clothes and she was sewing. They worked hard for everything they had, and they didn't have a whole lot.

"My father was Jewish and my mother was Italian," Rich continued, "and back in the 1950s that was almost unheard of. At first my dad's parents didn't accept the relationship, but that changed. I grew up in a rich tradition. One minute I'd be having a Seder meal and the next minute an Easter Sunday. I grew up on both sides—eating lox and bagels, and pasta on Sunday. It was an upbringing I wish everyone could have, because I learned about culture, about people, about family.

"As a kid, I liked to socialize with all different kinds of people," Rich went on. "That's one of the strengths I've carried over from my youth. Being able to relate to people is a very important part of who I am at Virtua."

In that role, Rich keeps his focus on the big picture and staying positive, another legacy of early experiences.

"I love what I do," he said. "I'm on the offense and I'm positive. It's never about 'woe is me.' I think too many people worry about things they can't control. You have to worry about the things you can control. Part of this attitude comes from nearly losing my life in an auto accident when I was 21. I had to work my way through college, and one night I was driving back from my job as a waiter in a restaurant in Gettysburg. I had a little '62 Volkswagen bug. I fell asleep at the wheel and hit a bridge abutment going about 40. Total kidney failure, total lung collapse.

"When you spend three weeks in a trauma unit near death, you don't worry about the small things anymore. You say to yourself, 'Don't waste a day.' My life is based on that philosophy. When I wake up in the morning, I'm looking forward to my day being something special. And my goal is to help other people get there too."

Miller has been CEO of Virtua for 15 years. He was chief financial officer and chief operating officer before moving up to lead the company. He's always worked in healthcare. For seven years before joining the company, he held financial consulting positions in the hospital industry.

Formed by the merger of two separate hospitals in 1998, Virtua is a comprehensive healthcare system headquartered in Marlton, N.J. Its mission is to deliver a world-class patient experience through programs in cancer treatment, cardiology, orthopedics, women's health, pediatrics, surgery, neuroscience, and wellness. Revenue has grown from $350 million in 1998 to $1 billion today. Virtua employs about 8,000 clinical and administrative personnel, and approximately 1,800 physicians serve as medical staff members.

"We deliver 7,600 babies a year," Rich said, "more than any other healthcare organization in our region. That's our lead service. We provide a lot of services related to women's health.

"We're also one of the few New Jersey hospitals that is financially healthy. We try to look at every program in terms of margin, so we can reinvest in our programs and people."

As CEO, Miller has had to institute many changes to get Virtua where it is today. Back in 2001, unhappy with the company's performance, he initiated a partnership with General Electric to get help.

"At the time, our quality and financial results were average," Rich said. "We hit the median in everything. I said to our managers at a meeting, 'I'd never want my kids to be called average. So we have to really change the way we think about what we do.'

"I called Jeffrey Immelt, Chairman of GE. He was just taking over from Jack Welch. I said, 'Jeff, I'd like to come up to see you and talk about some things. How much time could I have?' He said, 'It depends, Rich. If the idea is good, I'll spend a lot of time with you. If not, you've got about 15 minutes.'

"I said to myself, 'Great. I'm going to drive all the way to Fairfield, Connecticut and be on my way back after 15 minutes.'

"As it turned out, we spent an hour and a half talking about the things that GE brings to its customer base that could change the face of healthcare. After the meeting they sent out two of their master black belts to walk us through performance improvement. The light bulb went on and I said wow!"

Miller adapted GE's toolkit to address the problems he faced in health care.

"No industry has more fractured processes than our industry. We are the worst and we needed to look at that. We brought in GE's HR piece. We brought in their business models and other processes. We expanded the whole toolkit to change how we provide healthcare.

"We use the tools religiously at Virtua, but the key difference here is that it's driven from the top down. Every month our employees are presenting and I'm there asking questions, reinforcing what they're doing and helping them through the process. I'm making sure we're driving performance improvement throughout the organization. Too many health care organizations today, at the CEO level, say it's somebody else's job to do."

Rich spends as much time as possible interacting with employees.

"I meet with a cross section of about 30 employees on a monthly basis. They're at the ground level, the people who make it happen. We talk about everything from hand soap to what we're doing with the new hospital. It's their discussion. They'll throw something in the air, and I give them ownership of it. I'll hook them up with the right person, but it's their responsibility to come back with the right answer next month. I don't fix the problem. I ask them how they would fix it. They have the answer. They just haven't thought of it yet.

"And the next month they have the answer for me. When you have employees talking about the needs of the patient, you have them engaged. If they're talking about not having enough coffee in their work area, they're not engaged. At our last meeting everyone in that room was aligned. How can we help each other? How can we be better? What can we bring to the table to support our patients?"

I asked Rich what irks him.

"I very rarely lose my cool. Mistakes don't bother me. I make mistakes, everyone makes them. Just don't make a values mistake or an ethical mistake. Don't make a mistake where you're hurting your employee, or doing the wrong things, or kicking people in the pants. That angers me and my staff knows it."

Miller said he worries about his employees struggling economically, particularly female employees raising children alone. He's put together a company support group to provide clothing, meals, and other assistance.

How does he maintain balance?

"I work very hard Monday through Friday. When Friday comes, my wife and I go out to dinner and spend time together and I don't let anything interfere with that. And when my kids were growing up, I was on the soccer field every Saturday. If you don't have that balance, you're going to run into a problem along the way. I tell my senior management that I don't want to see their emails on Sunday afternoon. Have a life. Take your kids out. They're only going to be young for a short time."

Having made great strides in building and improving Virtua, Miller's vision for the future is clear.

"The future of medicine lies with technology and genetics, and enabling the patient to take better care of himself by having the right information. Patients are going to be more active in their care. The boomer generation has a much different mindset. We're a very active generation. We want to get our knees fixed so we can play basketball.

"I remember my mother coming out of the doctor's office with a prescription, and I'd ask her what it was for. She'd say, 'I don't know, but it must be okay because the doctor gave it to me.'

"My mindset is totally different. I'm caring for myself, I know what's best for me, and I'll make those decisions, not the physician. That's the generation that's coming into Virtua. How do we engage those people in a different way? That's what we're thinking about."

LEADING BY EXAMPLE

DAVE YOST, PRESIDENT AND CEO, AMERISOURCEBERGEN

Dave Yost's working class background influences almost every aspect of how he manages and leads AmerisourceBergen, a pharmaceutical wholesaler that employs about 10,500 people and posted revenues of more than $70 billion in 2008. Raised in Delaware, Dave's father was a diesel mechanic and his mother was a teacher's aide.

"Going to college," he told me, "was a pretty big deal." That's because Dave was the first in his family to do so.

"I think the guy at the top sets the tone for the organization," Dave continued, "not in an egocentric way, but the guy in charge has to walk the talk because people watch what you do versus what you say. I'm here at 6:30 in the morning. Could I do the job getting here at 8 a.m.? Yes, but I want people to know I'm here at 6:30.

"We don't fly around in corporate jets because this company operates on a very thin profit margin, and because I expect people to ride coach like I do. One of our salesmen came down the hallway one day and said to me, 'Geez, Dave, I didn't get in until 2 a.m this morning because my flight was cancelled.' And I said to him, 'Same thing happened to me the last time I flew to Denver.' I could relate to him because I'd been in the same situation, and that's a big part of leading a company. In my opinion, a lot of financial problems in our country result from a sense of entitlement that starts with the guy at the top."

AmerisourceBergen is headquartered in Valley Forge, Pa., with locations through the U.S., Puerto Rico, Canada, and the United Kingdom. It buys pharmaceutical and healthcare products from manufacturers, maintains large inventories in its warehouses, and delivers the products to drugstores, hospitals, chain stores, and physicians the day after they're ordered. This allows its customers to maintain small inventories and order quickly, according to demand.

"We're the classic middle person," Dave said. "The value we offer the manufacturer is that we bring their products to the marketplace in a very timely manner at the right price and manage the customer receivables. We help create the market for generic manufacturers, because we search for the best value products and make them available to our customers. For the customer, we get them the product on demand, so they can literally order tonight, get it tomorrow, and carry no inventory.

"We do a lot of volume," Dave went on, "north of $70 billion, but we work on incredibly thin margins. Our operating margin is 1.2%. Our net profit after tax is 0.75%. If you were to take a $100 bill and put three quarters on it, that's what we make—75 cents for every hundred dollars. Our gross profit is less than 3%, so we're running the whole company on less than 2%. This is a pennies and basis points business. I constantly remind all of our stakeholders not to be mesmerized by our revenues."

The roots of pharmaceutical wholesaling go back over 100 years and AmerisourceBergen is an amalgam of many companies. The present firm came into being in 2001 when AmeriSource Health Corporation merged with Bergen Brunswig Corporation. Yost was CEO of AmeriSource Health at the time.

"I've been a public company CEO for 48 quarters," Dave said. "Some people would say 12 years, but when you're a public company you talk in terms of quarters. My job is to produce both long term and short term results. Our compounded earnings per share have grown 16% during the last seven years."

Dave's father had been a flyer during World War II and he grew up wanting to be a pilot. He graduated from the Air Force Academy, but was not pilot qualified at graduation due to eyesight and depth perception issues. He then attended business school at UCLA. After five years in the Air Force, he went to work for a small family business in Ohio, the start of a 35-year career in pharmaceutical wholesaling.

Yost described his management style as "pretty egalitarian."

"I can tolerate a lot of things," Dave told me, "but not arrogance, either with customers, our suppliers, or with co-workers. That's the ego in play, and that's what gets a lot of companies in trouble. If the guy in the corner office thinks he's above it all, then his co-workers start thinking that way. If you're uncomfortable making your own coffee or making your own copies or carrying your own bag, you're not going to be comfortable at AmerisourceBergen. And you won't feel comfortable if you don't have a strong work ethic. We're very proud of the team we have."

Like most CEOs, Dave keeps in mind how families are affected by his decisions.

"It's a responsibility I take seriously because I come from a working class family. I know what it's like to live in a household when a job is in jeopardy. Again, it's a balancing act because you have to maintain your costs to survive, so we try to be balanced. We don't hire people at huge salaries, and we also don't do massive layoffs.

"Last year our healthcare costs went up, but we didn't pass it on to the employees. We didn't raise the employee contribution and we didn't cut benefits either. Everyone here has the same healthcare benefits. Since 2008 was a good year, we increased our voluntary contribution to the 401k."

AmerisourceBergen runs a Charitable Contributions Program that serves local institutions and agencies in communities where the company operates, through direct donations, volunteer support, and healthcare education. The program focuses on improving the mental, social, and physical well-being of the elderly.

Dave told me he's running the company on less absolute dollars than last year, due to a philosophy called CE2 (Customer Efficiency/Cost Effectiveness).

"Customer Efficiency means providing what the customer wants and needs, and Cost Effectiveness means doing it better than anyone else—not necessarily cheaper, but with more value.

"Three years ago we had a CEO, a COO, and five operating units. Today we still have a CEO, but no COO and three operating units. We've flattened the organization and are doing fine. I do the sales and marketing, and the CFO does the operations part in one of our units. You can't lower costs by laying off two people in the warehouse. You have to look at top level management when you're looking at managing costs, not just the middle and lower levels. So everyone's doing a bit more with less. I can ask people to do that because I'm doing it."

Does Dave find the job stressful?

"When your earnings and revenues are up, and you beat analysts' expectations, it's a fun job. When you're not meeting your expectations, it's not so much fun. But I can't tolerate CEOs who whine about the job.

Go look in the mirror, figure out what you have to do, and don't whine. At the end of the day you have no one to blame but yourself. You also have no constraints in the long term about how to fix the problems you're facing."

How does he stay grounded?

"I have a great wife, who keeps me humble. Sometimes I think she overachieves in that area. But seriously, someone's got to tell the emperor he has no clothes. How do I stay in touch? By walking around the company and being accessible. I answer my own phone, talk to customers, talk to suppliers, talk to analysts. And we do town hall meetings every quarter."

David adheres to the honor code of the Air Force: Don't lie, cheat, or steal, or tolerate those who do.

"People ask me, 'If someone cheats on his golf score, should you fire him?' Here's my answer. The people who lie on little things, lie on the big things. If they cheat at cards, they're going to end up cheating customers, and that's cheating you.

"Fast forward to our friends on Wall Street. They lied, cheated, and stole probably because they worked in an environment that tolerated it, even endorsed it. We're a straight arrow company around here. I make sales calls, so I understand sales puffery. But I also understand lies."

Asked about his legacy, Dave said, "My true legacy will be how the company survives after me. If this thing flounders a couple of years after I leave, then I didn't do my job right. That's why I feel CEOs shouldn't get payoffs until one or two years after they leave the company. Let's see how the organization does. If the CEO was maximizing profit for the short term and not the long term, if he was running the company to see what he could get out of it just before he left, he shouldn't get rewarded."

And for his advice to aspiring CEOs, Yost gave an answer that may surprise some.

"Having the objective of becoming a CEO will get you into trouble. Becoming a CEO happens by doing other things. And a lot of times it happens because of timing. When I talk to MBA students, I tell them that they have to accept timing as a key issue. You can be the greatest person, but the timing may not be right. If you didn't get a certain position, you probably weren't ready for it."

I asked Dave to expand on what he tells business students.

"First and foremost, enjoy what you do. If you enjoy what you do, you'll do it well and good things will happen. Take assignments you're not comfortable with, that stretch you a bit, but even then figure out how to enjoy them.

"Be sensitive to the work ethic and your use of time. This is especially important for young people. A lot of them want immediate gratification or don't want to put a lot of time into the job.

"I tell them, 'You've invested a lot of time already in college and grad school. Why don't you consider investing an extra 15 minutes or a half hour on the job every day?' My point is that older people like me have a different conception of time than generation X or Y. Instead of starting at 8 a.m. and leaving at 6 p.m. at the dot, why not come in 15 minutes early and leave a half hour later? That's 45 minutes a day that you're going to invest in your career, and it can be very productive time well spent.

"The third thing I tell them is to do their current job well. Don't look at any job as just a stepping stone. Don't say, 'I'm going to stay here a couple of years and then move on.' Do the job really, really well, then people will notice you. If you're only doing it until the next deal comes along, it may not come along.

"Finally, take the job seriously, but not yourself. If I get hit by a car tomorrow, AmerisourceBergen is going to make all its deliveries the next day and continue to do well. Arrogance and a sense of entitlement will always get you in trouble. A lot of people make AmerisourceBergen run— it's not just me and the people reporting to me.

"Having the right attitude is what helps differentiate you from your competitors," Dave concluded. "One of our customers is going to call us in a crisis at 5:30 p.m., saying they need a product at the last minute. It would be pretty easy for the person they reach to say, 'You should have ordered it yesterday, I'm out of here.' But in our company, someone is going to take care of the problem.

"Many of our products are the same as our competitor's, but our attitude is not. That's one of the values we offer."

THE CHANCE TO FAIL

ROBERT J. CIARUFFOLI, CEO, PARENTEBEARD LLC

When I asked Bob Ciaruffoli what makes CEOs tick, he smiled.

"I'd like to know that as well as you," he replied.

But it became quickly apparent during our conversation that Bob knows a great deal about leading companies and managing people, and he gladly shared that knowledge with me.

ParenteBeard (formerly ParenteRandolph), one of the top 40 certified public accounting firms in the country, was started in 1970 by Chuck Parente and John Randolph, who had both worked for Big Eight accounting firms. They borrowed space and equipment, and the company grew from two people in 1970 to 650 employees today. With headquarters in Philadelphia, the company's 15 offices are located predominantly in the northeast United States. Ciaruffoli joined the firm in February, 1979, and became CEO in January, 2000.

Bob told me the company is guided by two operating principles.

"The first is to perpetuate the business. Chuck and John, in their foresight, provided a tremendous opportunity for a lot of people, and we continue to believe that we have that obligation. In order to do that, you have to grow.

"The second principle, which came out of strategic planning sessions, was that we needed to focus our skill sets. We had a lot of people doing a lot of things. I was doing strategic planning for my clients, but I wasn't doing it for the clients of my other partners. There was no cross fertilization. We needed to institutionalize the business, in both industry and service niches. That's how we got into investment banking, forensic and litigation services, and other services." Bob has been instrumental in transitioning ParenteBeard from a northeastern Pennsylvania firm into a multi-state company.

Bob told me he never thought about becoming a CEO as a child. "When I was a kid, I had two things on my mind—working hard to make money, and having fun.

"Maybe I was forced into a leadership role," he said, "being the oldest of 10 children. It was a team environment, growing up."

Bob went to college for a year, then joined the Marines, which he calls "probably the best education" he ever had. After leaving the service he went back to school and took a job with a Big Eight accounting firm in Newark for four years, before joining ParenteBeard.

What was his track to the top?

"I think I was very fortunate. Chuck Parente saw something that I didn't necessarily see. He took me under his wing and gave me a lot of opportunity. He gave me a chance to fail. School prepares you somewhat, but in the real world you learn by making mistakes. You learn by doing and asking questions, and then asking still more questions.

"We've all made our share of mistakes," he continued. "When that happens, I tell people that's not the last mistake you're going to make or that I'm going to make. Back in 1980 I was a manager working on the account of the biggest client in the firm. And when I say the biggest client, I mean a very big and high profile client. It was a very complicated situation where you had separate accounting methods for financials, bookkeeping, and tax purposes. There were a lot of conversions.

"Long story short, we made a mistake. Chuck Parente had to go out and meet with the client, and we fixed the problem.

"That Saturday morning I walked into Chuck's office and said, 'Do you want my resignation?' He looked at me like I had two heads. He said, 'Bobby, what are you talking about?'

"I said, 'I screwed up big time on that client.'

"He said, 'What did you learn from it?'

"I told him what we did wrong and what I learned from it, and how I would deal with it the next time around.

"And Chuck said, 'That's not the last mistake you'll make in your career. The important thing is to learn from your mistake and not make the same mistake over again.'

"That really left an imprint on me and how I deal with people. It's one thing to make a mistake. That's acceptable. It's not acceptable to make the same mistake over and over again."

Today, very little of Bob's typical day is spent on the numbers side.

"With the size of the organization, my biggest client is now the firm. I focus on strategy and tactical issues. There are certain situations where I may get involved with clients, but that's usually from the strategic side.

"And the second area I focus on is coaching and mentoring, as opposed to fixing. It's generally easy to fix somebody else's problem, but what did you really accomplish? That person didn't learn anything in the process, and the next time they have a problem they're going to come back through my door. So I've lost an opportunity to teach them something and, more importantly, they lost an opportunity to improve their skills."

I asked Bob how he plans for inevitable leadership transitions in the company's future.

"Whatever we've collectively done to date is useless," Bob said, "unless we've developed strong leadership behind us. And I don't mean my replacement, because we already know who that will be. I mean who my replacement's replacement is going to be. And you ask that question for each critical position in the organization. It's not just identifying the person, but are they ready? What kind of training or skill sets do they need? How do we put them in positions so they have a chance to make mistakes and learn from them?"

To aid in leadership development, the company has implemented a training program called LEAP (Leadership, Entrepreneurship, and Achievement at Parente). Bob calls it a "tough, three-year program, the equivalent of getting an MBA." Run in affiliation with Penn State, the program selects 25 partners and managers from various regions and disciplines, through a "blind" application process. Participants bond in the program as they learn from the course content and each other's experiences.

I asked Bob what keeps him up at night.

"A partner or senior management team member who doesn't put up his or her hand and ask for help. We have a lot of bright people in this organization. We have the right answers among us. And nobody is that good that they know everything. Not even Chuck Parente. We work in a very fluid and changing environment, whether from a client or regulatory standpoint, so if someone doesn't ask for help, the chance of us getting into trouble increases significantly."

The other thing that keeps him up is the sense of responsibility he feels for the 650 families that depend on ParenteBeard.

"One of the questions we ask ourselves about everything we do, especially from a risk standpoint, is how does it affect 650 families? There's no way in the world I will ever let anything happen that jeopardizes this firm or the 650 families that depend on it."

For the future, Ciaruffoli envisions ParenteBeard expanding beyond its traditional market.

"Throughout most of our history we grew organically, by providing great service to clients. From 1970 through the mid-90s we spent nothing on marketing, as most business came through referrals. But as we moved out of northeast Pennsylvania, our brand recognition wasn't as great. Our goal now is to be the dominant regional firm in the mid-Atlantic region, from New York City to D.C. That's the five-year plan we're shooting for."

I asked Bob if he found his job grueling.

"It's a fun job," he said. "I have mostly good days, but every now and then you have not such a good day, like everyone else.

"I remember being interviewed by Chuck and John back in '79. We were in a ground level office and there was a road construction project going on outside. I forget the question I was asked, but I remember my response very well. It went along the lines of, 'I enjoy very much what I do, I work hard at what I do, and the day I have to drag myself out of bed to go to work is the day I look for another job. And if working on a construction crew is what makes me happy, that's what I'll do.' I haven't had to do that because I enjoy what I do. We work hard but we also have fun."

Summing up, Ciaruffoli called recent media criticism of CEOs "outrageous."

"Unfortunately, the news media focus on one or two high profile situations and paint the world with a broad brush. You clearly have some bad actors out there, but that's true of every aspect of life. Even if it was a hundred CEOs who were irresponsible, how many is that out of the thousands out there? There are a lot of great CEOs who take care of their organizations and people, and you never hear about them."

WORKING FOR LASTING SOCIAL CHANGE

JILL M. MICHAL, PRESIDENT AND CEO, UNITED WAY OF SOUTHEASTERN PENNSYLVANIA (UWSEPA)

Jill Michal, as President and CEO of United Way of Southeastern Pennsylvania (UWSEPA), is guiding her organization to have a lasting social impact in critical areas facing her region—education for children, income for families, and health for seniors. The organization serves more than 2.5 million people in Philadelphia and portions of Montgomery, Chester, and Delaware counties.

"In the education arena, we want to make sure that our kids enter school ready to learn through quality, early childhood education," Jill told me, "and that they stay on track to graduate from high school through quality interventions for at-risk kids. There are currently 73,000 youth in this region between the ages of 16 and 24 who are not in school and not working, and our focus is on getting them back in school or engaged in the workforce."

Another major focus is to provide families with jobs that pay a living wage, in industries that will grow over time.

"Our biggest challenge in this region, beyond unemployment, is underemployment," she told me. "A single parent with two school-age children living in the city of Philadelphia needs to earn roughly $48,000 to make ends meet without public assistance. That same individual working full time at minimum wage earns $14,870. That equation never works in the long term.

"But we also want to make sure we teach people not only the jobs skills they need to get a good job, but the life skills to keep it. We don't want people to become derailed if their child is sick or their childcare center is closed or they run into some personal life challenges."

In the health arena, UWSEPA focuses on seniors. Pennsylvania currently has the second oldest population in the country, and in less than ten years, depending on which study you read, Jill pointed out that it could become the oldest state in the country.

"Our social infrastructure is nowhere near being prepared to support that kind of growth," she said. "If we continue to put folks in nursing homes at the rate that we're currently going, the projection is that we'll be short about 50,000 beds.

"We tend to institutionalize older adults because we don't have a caregiver system that can support them aging with dignity and grace in their own homes. They can't do simple, daily tasks, like drive themselves to the doctor's office, or the pharmacy, or the grocery store. They can't do basic home repairs or shovel their walkways in the winter, but these very simple things don't warrant placement in a nursing home or a full-time attendant. Yet we don't have the infrastructure in place to support them to remain in their homes."

In trying to effect these kinds of social changes, I asked Jill how she measured success.

"About ten years ago, David Cohen, our board chair, challenged United Way to think differently about the way we did business. He said we had to make the shift from simply making grants, to truly making change. We agreed that we needed to think about how to rally a critical mass of diverse stakeholders around common causes, to drive lasting change.

"The next stage was to evaluate the organizations we support. Were they able to demonstrate that their interventions actually changed the trajectory of people's lives? That's how we're currently measuring our investment strategy, and we're developing tools to translate that to the broader community."

UWSEPA has about 80 staff and 12,000 volunteers. In 2008 they raised approximately $51 million from 112,000 people in 1,200 campaigns. In each of those campaigns, its pool of volunteers performed a range of tasks, from packing backpacks for homeless children, to collecting and distributing clothing, to delivering turkeys for Thanksgiving.

Michal grew up a little bit north of Allentown, Pa., in a small town called Schnecksville—"one of those towns that if you blink, you'll miss it," Jill said. After graduating from Penn State, she came to Philadelphia to start her career with Arthur Andersen in 1994 and stayed there until 2001. She started at UWSEPA as the Director of Finance, took on greater responsibilities over time, and became CEO in August, 2008.

But when the CEO position became available through her predecessor's departure, Jill wasn't sure at first she wanted to apply for the position.

"My kids at the time were very young, ages one and two. In addition, I wasn't sure I had the necessary fundraising experience. I made a very public announcement to our entire board that I was not applying for the job. I said, 'I'm devoted to this organization, but frankly I've spent my whole career spending money. I haven't raised five bucks in my whole life.'

"As I spent more time thinking about it, I realized that being a good fundraiser isn't some magical thing you do. It's about being passionate, being sincere, and being credible. If you can do those three things, you can sell something that you really believe in. In addition, a good colleague and my husband both encouraged me to apply for the position. That really was the turning point for me."

What made Jill shift from a public accounting company to a social service non-profit?

"My focus at Andersen was mostly healthcare, non-profits, and continuing care retirement communities. This was the area that I really had a passion for, and I love to give back. I wanted to keep my eye on how the bottom line produced for the community, not for somebody else's company."

Jill describes her leadership style as "collaborative."

"I really value getting things right over being right. I'm a facilitator and driver of change, but it's really more about getting people engaged and using their talents effectively to make that happen."

Finally, I asked Jill if being a woman helped or hurt in her leadership role.

"In this organization, it has no impact, especially since our staff might be 60% female at this point if not more. In my interactions with companies, I've never felt like anyone said, 'Oh, it's the woman CEO.' I've never felt labeled.

"I love this job," Jill concluded. "It's the most amazing thing I've ever done in my life, other than give birth to my two children."

TRANSPARENCY AND CARING

TIM ANDREWS, PRESIDENT AND CEO, ADVERTISING SPECIALTY INSTITUTE

"Think of anything that you can put a logo or a slogan on, to promote a company, product, achievement, or event," said Tim Andrews, President and CEO, as I sat across from him in his office. "T-shirts, mugs, pens, and key tags are popular examples.

"Let's say you're having a company picnic," Tim went on. "You might want a tablecloth, cups, napkins, and gift bags with your company logo. You can use one of our online tools to search among 750,000 products, to find the best price and match for what you want to do. The products are then imprinted on demand by one of our suppliers and delivered to you. ASI helps you create the whole palette for a marketing campaign."

ASI has served the advertising specialty market, also known as the promotional products industry, for over 50 years. The company has its home office in Trevose, Pa., employs about 500 people, and posted revenues of more than $60 million in 2008.

Andrews started out as a journalist at Dow Jones, publisher of *The Wall Street Journal*, then moved into a variety of marketing, technology, and business positions at the company. He next joined Primedia, where he ran the business-to-business publishing division. In 2002, Tim was recruited to join ASI, a family-owned Philadelphia company founded in the mid-1950s.

Did Tim imagine becoming a CEO as a child?

"I don't think I knew what a CEO was," Tim said. "I wanted to be a journalist. That was really my path, from five or six years old."

I wondered if Tim received formal business training beyond what he learned on the job.

"It was all on the job. I thought about going to Harvard Business School when I was about 30, after seven years as a journalist. But I couldn't really afford to go there. I grew up poor in rural Indiana. We were on welfare and food stamps, so what I had earned in New York was what I had earned in my entire life. I benefited from a lot of good internal programs at Dow Jones, and I also had a couple of good mentors."

Tim defines his role as CEO as "listening, and not only looking at financial statements. If a CEO thinks his job is to spend the day looking at financial statements, something is wrong there.

"About 40% of my job deals with talent management—developing and putting in place programs to manage and create incentives for my team. Another 30% of my time is spent with customers, mostly in their offices and at the 20 or so trade shows I attend every year. Of the last 30%, half is spent looking at other industries for ideas, and the other half is spent looking at the internal gauges of how the business is performing."

I asked Tim how he dealt with the climate of fear and uncertainty caused by the current recession.

"The challenge is to keep your employees focused, grounded in truth and not in fear. What we have now is a nation grounded in fear and not focused on the future. If everyone's afraid about what's going to happen, then it's going to happen. Yes, there are a lot of people without jobs, but at the end of the day 92% of people do have jobs. In a downturn, people are still spending money and you have to find out how to get that business."

Throughout our interview, Tim emphasized his role in fostering a corporate culture based on openness and transparency.

"What works for me is a quarterly all-company meeting, where I spend about 45 minutes talking through the major highlights of the last quarter, but also focusing on what's going to happen in the next few months," Tim said. "Then I take questions. I think we average 15 questions, which may not sound like that many, but they're pretty tough and educated questions. For example: 'Six months ago you told us we were really going to work on market share. How are we doing?' When you get a question like that in front of 450 employees, you know people are listening.

"When I joined the company six years ago," Tim recalled, "I told Norman Cohn, the owner, after he interviewed me, that I was going to say something to the employees and then take questions. I said I wanted to set the tone for an open-door policy.

"And Norman said, 'They don't ask questions at meetings.'

"And I said, 'They will, because I'm not going to leave until I get three.' And that's what happened. People weren't afraid to ask.

"You'll notice three windows in my office. It was a solid wall when I came here. On the first day I asked the building staff how long it would take to put in windows. People can know instantly when I'm here and when I'm not, just by looking in.

"If people have the sense over time that you're transparent and telling it like it is," Tim continued, "you've built a trust level where you can be honest with them, especially when bad times happen or you have to make a tough decision. If you can be honest with them about the little things and the good stuff, they'll know you're serious when there are also bad things to say."

Communication in any successful company is a two-way street. When I asked Tim what sets him off, he said, "Finding out bad news after the fact, when someone knew it in advance, or had a reasonable expectation it would happen. Number one, no CEO likes to be surprised. Number two, if I had known about the problem in advance, I could have avoided or limited the bad outcome, or made a different decision."

Sometimes a family business can be reluctant to turn over the reins to an outsider. This wasn't the case at ASI.

"Norman and his family said I would make every business decision. That doesn't mean that I don't ask for advice and that it's not widely supplied. Everyone has different viewpoints, and I consider them as I decide on the best course of action. Never have I been told by the family that I couldn't do something, even if other people didn't agree."

ASI has grown impressively since Andrews came on board six years ago. The company has increased its distributor members from 17,000 to 23,000, while growing the supplier network to 3,600. Its online marketing system, ESP Online, now has 33,000 users, up from 5,000 a few years ago.

"I think we have a great opportunity to grow the number of distributors, to perhaps 40,000, in five to eight years. We've moved into Canada in the last two years. It's a significant market, and we have other opportunities around the world."

I asked Tim how he views his legacy.

"I think a legacy is created by a series of actions, and only becomes clear after the CEO is no longer around. I try to help people be the best they can be. I'm not sure that's a legacy, it's more a style. If I can do that, I'll feel really good.

"I don't look at this as a collection of 500 employees, but as 500 families that are depending on our decision-making," he went on. "Right now I'm going through what every CEO goes through, and that's the renewal of our health insurance. It's probably one of the largest costs that employers look at. There are salaries, payroll taxes, and then healthcare. How do we fairly manage that increase?

"We had five healthcare scenarios to choose among this year, and we immediately eliminated three because I couldn't stand in front of my employees at an all-company meeting and feel comfortable explaining those options, given the culture we want to continue to have."

When I asked Tim what he was most proud of, he brought it back to ASI's culture.

"When I joined the company, one of the siblings said, 'You're working for a family business. What does that mean to you?'

"I gave a stumbling answer because I had never been CEO of a family business. Two years passed before I was finally able to answer the question: we care. We may not always be able to keep every employee and we don't tolerate underperformance. However, we make decisions from a caring perspective, and that's good.

"I think it's really important to give back. You can run an organization with a heads-down, bottom line approach. Or you can take the heads-up approach, which is what the Cohn family does. We've done a tremendous amount to get the company involved in charitable work. Every holiday season we have an adopt-a-family program through the local homeless shelter at the American Red Cross. We ask employees to volunteer, and they buy toys and clothing for children and families with their own money. Last year about 80% of the employees volunteered for the program. We helped about 60 or 70 kids have a great holiday season.

"And we give out a free turkey to every employee during the holidays," Tim added. "When we did a survey of employees, 93% said don't mess with the turkey. So the turkey is safe."

PERPETUATING A WORK ETHIC

MIKE PEARSON,
PRESIDENT,
CONTEMPORARY
STAFFING
SOLUTIONS, INC.

What stood out for me in my interview with Mike Pearson was the way he embodies and carries forward the work ethic he learned from his mother, Donna, who founded Contemporary Staffing Solutions in 1994.

"My mother was a single mom who raised five kids," Mike told me. "We didn't have much money at all. Growing up it was week-to-week, paycheck-to-paycheck. There were a lot of sacrifices back then, but my mother never gave up. It was her strong work ethic and her integrity that I learned from.

"There are some people within our industry who are very ethical and have high integrity," Mike went on. "And then there are other people in our industry, like any industry, who look at their pockets first. My mother always said, 'Be honest with your customers and treat your employees fairly.' We always remember where we came from."

Contemporary, which specializes in placing temporary workers in various industries, posted revenues of $31.3 million in 2008. The company, headquartered in Mt. Laurel, N.J., has eight offices in New Jersey, Pennsylvania, Delaware, and Florida, and about 900 temps out on assignment at any one time.

Having grown up in a business family and witnessed his mother's success firsthand, Pearson was always interested in becoming an entrepreneur. He majored in business and marketing at the University of North Carolina, Charlotte, and in his senior year took all his classes at night so he could work during the day as a salesman for United Parcel Service. Hired by UPS full time after graduation, Pearson's next career stop was at a small company selling life insurance software.

"I covered 22 states, selling to home offices," he said. "I learned a lot at that company."

Mike joined his mother's firm in 1996, working with one of his brothers to open a Delaware office, the company's third at the time.

"We both took a massive pay cut to come here," he recalled. "My mother always had the philosophy that we weren't going to take a step up until we earned it. So my brother and I started out cold-calling, running a desk, breaking our teeth on the staffing side of the house."

When Mike's mother passed away in 2001, he became partners with his siblings. They worked together for the next few years. Eventually, Mike's brother stepped down as president to follow other pursuits and Mike took over his role.

Asked about his typical day, Mike said, "You always try to have a plan every day. I want to make sure I'm talking with customers, managers, and even people below managers to make sure things are going well. You can't ignore any areas.

"Being a CEO is more grueling than glamorous," he continued, "not like the TV shows. You'll have a month or two of pure excitement and growth, and then it all explodes on you, and you say to yourself, 'How did that happen? I didn't see it coming.' So I always say, don't get too comfortable."

To ensure that employees are performing well, the company has "win/win performance agreements" with each worker.

"You have clearly outlined expectations for each manager and employee," Mike explained. "You've got numbers tied into that, and specific tasks that need to be done each week, each quarter, and throughout the entire year. You outline all the expectations and sign off on that. Then you can constantly go back and revisit that agreement to make sure employees are performing. For example, 'You said you were going to have team training on the third Friday of the month. I notice you're not having it and it's in your win/win agreement. What's happening?'"

Asked how his employees would describe him, he responded: "A good listener, a good team builder, solution oriented. Doesn't point the finger at anyone unless he points it at himself first."

Pearson advises aspiring CEOs to plan carefully and make sure they have mentors to help guide them.

"A lot of people say they're going to start a business, and have the attitude that they're just going to do it. Well, you need a very clear plan of how it's going to be done and two or three mentors you can bounce the ideas off of."

Mike said using fellow CEOs as mentors improves him as a leader.

"Inside our industry there are a lot of common problems, issues, and strategies. The most knowledge I've ever gotten is from leaders of similar, non-competing companies. I can use these CEOs as a sounding board. I can say, 'I've got an issue and need some help. Can we get on the phone?'"

Mike is most proud of the teams he's hired, trained, and built. He was gratified by a recent phone call from the first employee he hired, who worked for him for five years.

"She called me one day and said, 'I just wanted to thank you for all the training you provided me. You knew that as we grew, the company would also grow. I'm a star performer where I work now because of all the training you gave me.'"

Mike says his legacy is to build on the foundation that his mother set in place.

"When a business passes to a new generation, it's usually either sold very quickly or fails very quickly," he said. "My legacy is that I've worked with my siblings and partners to continue the same work ethic and integrity of my mother. I don't look for awards. I want to continue the growth of the company and see employees be productive here.

"Our strategy is to make sure we position ourselves in the right niches for staffing," he went on, "and continue to make changes as a company, because if you become stagnant, you run the risk of running yourself right out of the business. Some people are okay if they shrink. We don't want to shrink. We want to grow with the industry and educate ourselves about other staffing models out there."

Pearson believes that problems in companies develop when they get too big and forget about their employees.

"I had a friend at Enron. He was only there six months. He was told he was going to retire there, that he would be making a million a year. Six months later the whole thing exploded. Hearing his story was painful.

"I blame part of this on the government, and part on CEOs and leadership teams. This company is nothing without our employees. If more companies had that philosophy, you wouldn't see a greedy mindset."

Asked for his final thoughts, Mike gave this advice:

"Outside of hard work, be patient and celebrate the little victories. Don't get caught up in thinking you're going to be Bill Gates in a year or two and ruling the world. Life is too short. Enjoy your friends and family, and stay positive."

PRESERVING JOBS IN A GLOBAL ECONOMY

DR. JEFFREY GRAVES, CEO, C&D TECHNOLOGIES

"Quite frankly, as a kid, leadership to me came very naturally," Jeff Graves told me, "but I never thought about leading things in the future. It was probably 20 years before I realized I had learned leadership skills as a youth that helped my career in a lot of ways."

What Graves didn't realize at the time was how much he learned from playing football while growing up in Indiana.

"I was always a fairly small kid, so I had to work harder than anyone else. In high school I not only made the varsity team as a sophomore, but also became captain of the team when I was a senior. I started on both offense and defense, and I made all state in both directions. We also won the state championship in my senior year. It was a tremendous run.

"We had no great athletes on the team, including me, but we won every game, and our closest margin was about 24 points. We blew everyone away, and that was because of excellent teamwork. Nobody was in it for himself, everyone wanted to win, and it didn't matter what it took to get over the goal line.

"That was the seed of my leadership skills—learning how to influence people. When you're the captain of the team you have no authority with the other kids, but they look to you for subtle direction. You learn to lead by influence, but that didn't dawn on me until 20 years later when I reflected on it."

Another huge influence was the example Jeff's parents set.

"Neither of my parents went to college. They both worked for Indiana Bell, which was part of AT&T, and made their way up into fairly high management positions based on their wits and hard work. My mom died from cancer when I was 15 years old, and until two weeks before her death she went to work every day, commuting about 45 minutes into the center of Indianapolis. We didn't talk about it, but that was just the expectation—you were sick, but still you got up and went to work."

Graves earned undergraduate and graduate engineering degrees at Purdue and the University of Wisconsin, respectively.

"I thought I was going to be an engineer my whole life. I enjoyed it and thought I would run an engineering organization some day.

"The biggest influence on my career was Jack Welch. When I left college I went to work for Rockwell, which was a wonderful environment modeled on GE—very big on the empowerment of people, particularly young people. You got ridiculous amounts of responsibility very early on, because they pushed authority down into the lower levels of the organization. So I grew up there for five years. GE was a subcontractor undergoing changes under Jack Welch, and I was brought into the organization.

"I was given a lot of responsibility and there weren't many safety nets. GE took chances on people. They gave you a lot of rope, but you could also hang yourself with it. It was a wonderful training ground. I went through the engineering and manufacturing parts of the company. Then I moved into running the business side of things."

Jeff eventually left GE to head a $400 million electronics firm, replacing a CEO who was retiring. Brought in to restructure the business, the experience left a profound impression on him.

"It was a brutal transition," he recalled. "After 2000, the electronics business was crashing. We were a public company and people could see the financials. They knew we had to do it, but it was still brutal. We had to let go of a few thousand people in manufacturing positions in the states. The company was located in a fairly small town, Greenville, S.C., so it was the people in the community who you knew and their children.

"One night I took my wife and children out to dinner and we chatted with the young lady who waited on us. She told us she had to drop out of a major university and come back to the local community college because her dad had just been laid off from his job. It turned out that he was laid off by my company."

The experience affected Graves in a number of ways. First, he makes sure not to isolate himself from employees when layoffs are inevitable.

"When we do major layoffs, I always do a number of them myself. When you have to sit across from someone who's angry and crying, you say, 'Never again is this going to happen on my watch. I'm going to do everything I can to avoid this.'"

You do that, he believes, by looking at strategic planning with a broad sense of responsibility.

"If a CEO waits too long to make changes, the step down can be huge and painful. Some global changes are just going to happen. Electronics has gone to Asia. Probably nothing was going to save that in the states. But if this electronics company had started a transition ten years earlier and invested in new products, maybe they could have replaced those jobs. I sit on two outside boards, and most of the CEOs I know feel it's a deep personal tragedy when you have to downsize and restructure a company."

When Graves joined C&D Technologies in 2005, he said, laughing, "The honeymoon period was over before I even started."

Based in Blue Bell, Pa., C&D Technologies is a 100-year-old company that produces and markets electrical power storage and conversion products, including industrial batteries, high frequency switching power supplies, and converters. These products provide reliable backup power for critical infrastructure, such as telecommunication systems, data centers, computer rooms, bank and financial systems, and many other applications.

About a decade before Graves arrived, the company tried, unsuccessfully, to diversify into electronics. This resulted in an under-invested and demoralized power storage business, a new business that was struggling. Banks were banging on the door. Deeply in debt, C&D Technologies was highly leveraged.

"My first priority was to get the businesses running better daily, and then figure out strategically what we were going to do as a company."

Graves got things cleaned up, refinanced the company's debt, sold the electronics business to a Japanese firm, and reinvested the money back into the core business. Jeff is proud that fewer than a dozen people lost their jobs during the transition. C&D Technologies returned to profitability in the first quarter of 2008.

Jeff's core strategy as CEO is to focus on the customer.

"The magic that I learned at GE about keeping a business healthy is to be very close to your customers in a coordinated way, to the point where you go out and get candid feedback, not just from the president of the division you're selling to, but from your sales guys on the street and their customers. Some things you're good at, and some things you're not. If you can stay close to that customer, you have a shot at changing in time, in order to grow. I have my manufacturing leader and plant managers go on the road to where our products are delivered. They see our products come off the truck, and then ask the guys installing them if they have any frustrations and what they need from us.

"Then our guys come back to the office and we talk about it: what are we doing well and what are we not? Where is our customer going to be in a few years, and what do we have to offer? Maybe it's a new service or a new product to keep up with changing technology. We make lead acid batteries today, but lithium is coming along and, in five years, may totally displace what we do. Are customers interested? Why would they buy that product over what we have now? If you put the focus on the customer, everybody wins.

"A CEO I respect said on TV that his employees are number one. It's an easy thing to say and I agree with it in my heart of hearts, but the way to retain employees in a growing company is to make your customer number one.

"And the other piece, which goes back to my football days, is that you have to be able to elicit and share ideas from everyone in an open, non-defensive way. I have a few good ideas, but so do my sales guy, my manufacturing person, and my technology guy. If you can create an atmosphere where ideas, good or bad, are thought about, worked on, and accepted, you can go a long way. If you do that and touch the customer, generally you'll make good decisions and not be surprised by the future. If you miss either one of those, you can be dead in the water."

Jeff's experiences with downsizing and turnaround situations afford him a long-term vision of what will best sustain C&D Technologies in a changing world.

"We have a plant in Milwaukee where we have invested in a lot of capital equipment. I was out there one night talking to the employees on the third shift. Most of them were thanking me, saying you came here three years ago, you told us you cared, and you invested in the business.

"One employee in the back, who seemed in his 30s, said, 'How about taking some of that money you spend on equipment and giving us bonuses?'

"And I said to him, 'I understand why you feel that way, but if we run our business right, our products will be needed for decades. I could give you a one-time bonus, but if we put this new equipment on the floor, not only can you finish your career here, but your kids will have jobs here paying $20 an hour.'"

Graves views his legacy in the same vein.

"I love going to our production facilities in Mexico and China. But at the same time I'm an American, and would love to see a business that's sustainable in America as well as around the world. We want to be a global leader in energy storage, but I want to make sure a key piece of that remains in North America."

SECURING THE SHIP

MICHAEL BARRY, CHAIRMAN, CEO, AND PRESIDENT, QUAKER CHEMICAL CORP.

Mike Barry's first day as chief executive officer of Quaker Chemical was an eventful one. He took the reins of the company in October 2008, "just as the world fell apart."

"I'll never forget sitting here on the first day, and all these reports were coming in about our customers canceling their orders," Mike recalled. "For the first nine months of 2008 we were on track for record revenue, earnings, and cash flow. When the financial crisis happened, basically everything stopped. Our industries were hit very badly and our volumes were down about 35% virtually overnight. That's huge for a manufacturing company that has a heavy service orientation.

"All the planning I'd done for my first 90 days literally went out the window," Mike said. "We had to react pretty quickly to get through this."

A 90-year-old company listed on NYSE (KWR) and headquartered in Conshohocken, Pa., Quaker produces chemical products and services to aid manufacturers who work with industrial metal.

"If you produce steel, or have to drill, grind, or mold metal, you generally use chemicals to aid in that process," Mike told me, "as well as to clean off old chemicals and keep products from rusting. Our products don't end up in the final product, but they help the process run more smoothly.

"Our big customers are the steel, auto, and appliance companies. The cost of our products and services is relatively small, but we make a big difference in the cost structure of how companies produce parts.

"We're small in the scheme of companies," Barry noted. "Revenue in 2008 was a little under $600 million. But at the same time we're very complex, very global. We're in basically every country around the world, with 1300 employees."

In the midst of the economic meltdown, Mike said his first order of business was "to get through the night and secure the ship."

"We undertook two major cost reduction efforts and then we increased our margins back to acceptable levels. We had to make sure we were generating cash. I worked with our teams to make sure we had the right actions in place. I was traveling and talking to our key leaders, making sure everybody understood our priorities, but also using that time to tell them, 'Hey, we're in good shape here. It's a tough situation, but we're going to get through it. Just hang in there. We're going to be fine.'

"We lost big in the fourth quarter of 2008, but got back to breakeven in profitability in the first quarter of 2009. The second quarter we made good money—maybe not quite as much as the previous year, but not that far away. By the fourth quarter we were able to produce record profits despite our volumes still being down. We generated a record cash flow in 2009 and paid down our debt 26%. So we stabilized everything, and now a lot of my time is focused on strategically positioning Quaker for the future. We feel it's a good time to make acquisitions. I've been spending my time talking to other companies."

Barry became CEO after 10 years of serving as chief financial officer and in executive business roles at Quaker. Asked about the main difference between the roles, Barry replied, "The buck stops here. The vision for the company stops at this one place.

"I think there are three keys to running a good business," he went on. "You have to have a good strategy, and you need to actively involve your team in developing strategy. You have to have good people throughout the organization. I made some changes in that area when I came on board. And then you have to be able to execute very well, and have good processes and systems in place to reach your goals. We've kept our strategy, but made some changes in organizational structure to make sure we executed well."

Barry grew up in Drexel Hill, Pa., and, except for a couple of years, has lived his whole life in the Philadelphia area. He studied chemical engineering at Drexel University and then earned an MBA from Wharton. He previously worked for Arco Chemical.

As a child, he showed an entrepreneurial spirit.

"I was a good student, always trying to make money in some fashion. I sold lemonade, did work for people, and was a paperboy. I put myself through school. I've always had a strong work ethic.

"My first job coming out of school was working in a refinery for Mobil Oil. After a couple of years I realized I wanted to get more into the business side of things, rather than be an engineer, and I got a MBA. I never thought I wanted to be the president of a company someday.

"I always get concerned when people in a new job start thinking automatically about their next job," Mike told me. "Don't think too far ahead. Just concentrate on your current job, do well, and make a difference in what you do today. If you continue to excel in what you currently do, you'll get opportunities to grow in the future. I've been fortunate through the years to have had good bosses who empowered me to take on different responsibilities and try new things."

Mike said that Quaker's close relationship with customers is different from its competitors.

"We employ the 'customer intimacy model.' It's a consultative and proactive approach to dealing with customers. When they have issues and need them to be solved, they come to Quaker.

"If a customer needs to produce more steel, we help them create a solution. We understand their needs at a very technical level and we'll translate that back to the lab. We'll provide a product for them that they'll be able to sell both on the floor of the mill, as well as high up in purchasing.

"Our mindset is geared towards making our customers more profitable, even if it ends up hurting us. We'll recommend that they can get by with less of our product or maybe we'll suggest a better product out there than ours. We're willing to do that because it increases our credibility with our customer base, and helps us increase our market share over the long term."

How would Mike's employees characterize his management style?

"I think they would say I'm tough but fair, somebody who establishes fair goals, gives direction, and involves the team.

"We just had an incident this week," Mike said, "where one of my guys did something I just wasn't happy about. I let him make the decision, but later we had a discussion. I gave him my perspective and coaching, because I think the important thing is to learn and go forward.

"He was receptive to my feedback and said, 'You're right. I should have looked at the situation a little differently.' I try not to be a micromanager or too prescriptive ahead of time. If it's not a critical decision, I let people make their own judgments and, if I disagree, we'll talk about it."

I asked Mike about one or two key decisions he made as CEO that turned out to be good moves over the last year. He mentioned decisions he made during the financial meltdown that got Quaker back to a profitable level pretty quickly.

"When crude oil was $150 a barrel, our raw material costs were going through the roof. We're selling to auto and steel companies, people who don't want to hear about price increases. But we had to pass on very large price increases to our customer base. It was the last thing they needed, but we were able to get that through and not get killed by raw materials. When the volumes dropped off, that really helped set the stage for getting our margins back to acceptable levels. In the process, we really learned a lot about our value to our customers. It goes back to customer intimacy, the relationships we have.

"The other key was cutting costs early. We said, 'Okay, this is not going to get better, it's not going to come back fast, we need to act now.' Again, both of those decisions were made ahead of our industry. Other competitors didn't do it and now they're really struggling. They can't get prices up because things are so bad. They waited too long to take action."

For the future, Barry wants Quaker "to grow substantially. There's consolidation needed in our industry and we believe we should be a leader in that, through both organic growth as well as through acquisitions. Our goal is to be a billion dollar company within five years."

Asked about recent CEO abuses, Mike said, "I'm always amazed at how these banks and Wall Street firms are still giving out huge bonuses. I have a friend who works for a local company that went through bankruptcy, and all the executives got huge bonuses for just hanging around during that period. I don't understand it.

"At the end of 2008, we were losing money big time. But it was still, overall, a good year for us, and we would have normally paid out at least some bonuses. I recommended to the board that we pay no bonuses at all.

"The board initially pushed back but they went with my recommendation. We were in survival mode. I just didn't think it was the right thing to do in our situation, and the people in our organization really didn't expect them either. A board member later told me that when he hears stories about CEO greed, he always points out Quaker Chemical as an example of the opposite."

MAKING THE RIGHT BETS

DAVID J. ADELMAN,
PRESIDENT AND CEO,
CAMPUS
APARTMENTS, INC.

When David Adelman was 11, he was playing basketball with a family friend named Alan.

"I said to him, 'I bet I can beat you,'" David recalled. "And Alan replied, 'Oh yeah? I'm going to teach you a thing or two about betting.' He whipped my butt and took everything from me. I lost my basketball, football, baseball glove, and bankbook. I had to go to his office every Saturday and stack lumber until I earned it all back. My parents thought it was a real character-building experience."

The man who taught Adelman a hard lesson about betting was Alan Horwitz, who founded Campus Apartments in 1958.

"I had my Bar Mitzvah two years later," David continued. "I had about $2000 in gift money. I gave it to Alan and became a limited partner in his company at 13. I'd come down to his building and sweep the hallways and thought it was the greatest thing. As I grew up I learned the whole business, doing maintenance jobs, painting apartments, doing leasing and accounting. It's the only job I've ever had, except for a couple of summers making hoagies and working at a marina."

Adelman is now CEO of Campus Apartments and Horwitz, his partner, is chairman.

The company is one of the nation's largest developers, owners, and managers of student housing, with over $1 billion in assets under management, more than 21,000 beds in 17 states, and serving over 50 colleges and universities. Campus Apartments has almost 600 employees and revenues are about $70 million. Dave calls Horwitz "a real visionary in building quality housing for college students, so parents feel good about leaving their kids."

"There's not a university around that still does its own food service," Adelman explained. "It's the same concept with housing. Universities are asking themselves: why are we building housing when someone else can do it more efficiently? The university becomes our client and we solve their housing problems.

"Part of what we do is build housing on a university's land. The other part is nuts and bolts real estate—going into an area that lacks quality housing, buying a building, fixing it up, marketing it accordingly, and renting it to college students."

As a mentor, Alan Horwitz has taught Adelman many things.

"But the most important thing he taught me was to love what you do," David said. "It shouldn't feel like work. If it's a grind, you're going to burn out. The only thing that gets you through the tough times is knowing that you've had such a good time doing it, and that it's impossible not to have a bump in the road. That kind of momentum will carry you through everything. You also need to appreciate what you've already accomplished, instead of being caught up in growth, growth, growth."

Adelman, 37, gradually transitioned into the CEO role about 12 years ago.

"I didn't know exactly where I would take the company. It was a small mom and pop Philadelphia business at that time. We had 30 employees when I first started. I helped modernize things and put in systems and procedures, focusing on the capital structure, financing, and bringing in more sophisticated products to finance our business.

"The real transition point was the late 1990s and early 2000s, when the University of Pennsylvania asked us to take over property management for their off-campus portfolio. They owned about 1,000 apartments in 77 buildings. It was the first big disagreement my partner and I had.

"Alan said to me: 'What do you want to be a fee guy for? We're owners. We don't want to manage someone else's property. Then we'll have to deal with their headaches and their tenants calling us.'"

But Adelman felt it was a bet worth making, and he turned out to be right.

"I told Alan that if we could do a good job for Penn, and learn how to do the back office to report to an institutional owner like that, we could do it for anybody. It turned out I was right and other universities started calling us."

In the years since, Campus Apartments has experienced broad growth and demand. To raise capital, they launched a $1.1 billion venture in 2006 with GIC RE, the Government of Singapore's Real Estate Investment Arm, geared toward the acquisition, development, and consolidation of university-related real estate.

"We're private, with a high profile global partner. They're hands off and we have full discretion over their capital. There are two larger public companies in the U.S. that do what we do, but we're the largest private company in the country that does this kind of business."

Adelman, who grew up on the Main Line right outside of Philadelphia, showed leadership qualities during his undergraduate years at Ohio State, where he majored in finance and political science.

"In college I was president of my fraternity house. They had a $150,000 deficit when I took over, and I left with $50,000 in the black. So I was already figuring stuff out. I graduated from college on Thursday and showed up here on Monday to start working. I didn't take a year off to go to Europe with my friends."

Although Adelman received a lot of mentoring from Alan Horwitz, he often had to figure out things on his own. It's inevitable, he said, that a CEO makes mistakes.

"I once lost a pretty big deal because I didn't like the guy sitting on the other side of the table. After it fell apart, Alan said to me, 'You weren't going golfing with the guy. What does it matter if you don't like him? If you liked the deal and it was an honest deal, who cares?'

"You have to take chances and make mistakes. You can't be cautious. I just make sure we don't make them twice. And come clean when you make one, so I don't end up reading about it."

For the future, Adelman's strategy is "to continue the smart growth. We're somewhat recession proof in this business because people are always going to college, but it's a good opportunity to look at your organization and make sure you have the right people. When times are good, you don't look around to see how you can improve the business. There's no excuse to stand for mediocrity."

Over the years, Adelman has changed his attitude about managing employees.

"I certainly wasn't Jack Welch, getting rid of the lowest 10% every year. I probably was more on the loyal side—if you're here, you're here forever. And now I don't know if that's right either. It's best to be somewhere in between. I always say to my people, it's easy to fire somebody, it's a lot harder to train someone and make it work. I don't give up on people. There are some people where I say this isn't working, but first I want to give someone a chance.

"I've transformed from being a micromanager ten to fifteen years ago, to realizing I've got guys and women smarter than me. I think I finally woke up one day and said, 'You can't do it all by yourself.' That's the not the right way to do things. Either you trust the people you work with or you get new people. I think the employees feel better. I say to them, 'I'm going to check on you and drive you nuts on certain things, but go ahead and do your stuff.'"

Finally, I asked David about the values that drive the company.

"I have little kids and I said to them, 'You only get one reputation.' For us, it's doing the right thing by our investors, our clients, and our customers. And our customers include the parents of the students we serve. I'm entrusted with people's children. When I speak at our managers' meeting, I say to them, 'You're responsible for other people's children. It's the highest privilege someone can give you.'"

FINDING OPPORTUNITY IN CRISIS

CRISTÓBAL CONDE, PRESIDENT AND CEO, SUNGARD

After studying astronomy and physics at Yale, Cris Conde started a small company in 1983 with two other men from Philadelphia.

"The company had one office in New York and one in Philly," Cris told me. "One day the three of us were talking, and we agreed that if we were really successful someday we'd have eight employees, including the three of us. Then I ran out of money. I couldn't afford New York anymore, and one of my partners had a friend in Philadelphia who sublet her dining room to me. So I set up a cot in her dining room and took the train to New York every other day."

The company Cris co-founded, Devon Systems International, eventually did very well, and was acquired by SunGard in 1987. Cris stayed on and slowly moved up in the ranks. When SunGard decided to expand in Europe, Conde became part of that assignment.

"We had one person there, so I became the second. I opened 13 offices and hired close to 2,000 people in Europe. I lived there about seven years, then came back, got promoted, and eventually became CEO."

With revenues of about $5.6 billion in 2008, SunGard is one of the world's leading software and IT services companies, providing software and processing solutions for financial services, higher education, and the public sector. SunGard also provides disaster recovery services, managed

IT services, information availability consulting services, and business continuity management software. It serves over 25,000 customers in more than 70 countries. Headquartered in Wayne, Pa., SunGard has 20,000 employees worldwide, with about 2,000 based in the Philadelphia area.

SunGard went public in 1986 and remained a public company until August 2005.

"We took the company private in 2005 through a leveraged buyout," Conde said. "It was at the time the largest tech LBO ever. Seven investors each kicked in $500 million in equity, and then we went out and borrowed $8 billion, so it was an $11.5 billion deal. These guys are very smart and very data driven. It's all about performance. We pay no attention to the ups and downs of quarterly results. We pay more attention to the long term. You still have to make a tradeoff between the short term and the long term, but we can favor the long term to a greater degree. It worked out very well. We're growing roughly three times faster than when we were a public company. We feel we have more access to capital now."

But SunGard is not impervious to business cycles, with revenues and earnings flat in 2009. Part of being a CEO, Cris told me, is making sure employees stay focused during tough times.

"People freeze when they encounter something unanticipated. While that's a natural reaction, my job is to get them to think things through and act. How do we turn this economic crisis into the biggest opportunity of our careers? When you look at the great crises, they've all resulted in great transfers of wealth and power, as long as you survive it and stay in the game. If you leave the game or decide to go into a different direction, then you lose the opportunity to correct.

"The losers will blame it on the crisis, which to me makes no sense at all because we all went through the same crisis. It's not the crisis. It's what companies did or didn't do during the crisis. It's whether or not they went into the crisis overstretched. The people who were going for the quick buck didn't have any reserves."

Conde grew up in Santiago, Chili, and came to the U.S. with his parents in the mid-70s. He attended public high school outside Washington, D.C. and then went to Yale, where he had "a lot of fun" studying astronomy and physics.

"I love tinkering and I love math, and you get to do the two in physics. The kind of astronomy I was studying was all math, black hole theory. I was one of the first physicists who came to Wall Street. I think math and the physical sciences are much more important than classic business study. They're all about problem solving, and I think that's incredibly helpful."

Conde's management style is to allow his employees the same independence and opportunity that he values as a leader.

"If you want to hold people accountable, you need to leave them alone to achieve results. The last thing I need is for somebody to say, 'Well, Cris, the reason why I didn't make my budget is because I was doing all these things you asked me to do.' So you have to bite your tongue and not tell them what to do.

"The people who work for me directly, there's very little I can teach them. But two to three levels below them, I can make a difference. I reach down into the organization but I don't tell them what to do. I tell them, 'Look, this is what I think. Now, feel free to totally disregard this.' I have to say it about five times before they actually understand that I'm quite okay with them disregarding me.

"At the end of the year you get to measure whether they achieved what they said they would do. If not, there's no reason why you should pay a bonus. Most companies are probably afraid to not pay for lack of performance. And then you see these horrible scandals in the papers."

Conde values feedback and contributions from his colleagues and staff, since "people who've been in a company for a long time become totally inbred."

"When we took the company private I heard everybody's opinion, but in the end that was my decision. But there have been only a handful of decisions that I've made like that.

"Someone told me that we should take certain steps to grow our professional services. I said, 'That's never going to work.' The idea stayed in the back of my head and three months later I said, 'It's a crazy idea that guy gave me, but let's give it a shot.' We did it and grew fantastically. Other people's ideas can add a lot of value."

Like every CEO I interviewed for this book, Conde has made a few left turns that should have been right turns.

"I tell employees that one of our core values is taking pride in doing things the right way, not the short way. My single biggest mistake was in violating that core value in one of the largest acquisitions I made, about 15 years ago. I took short cuts in due diligence. Everything that went bad with that business was there to be seen, but I chose not to see it. I had blinders on because I was so enamored with the technology, with the people, with the whole glitz of the business. So we made the acquisition and promptly flushed the $300 million we spent on it.

"I talk about it all the time because it was a very expensive lesson. I might as well leverage the tuition that I paid, right? I say, 'Look, in the end, the single biggest failure is not when you paid 5% too much, it's when you shouldn't have bought at all.'

"And the same thing is true when you run a company. It's not so much optimizing how the company does something. It's recognizing and avoiding the things that shouldn't be done at all. Who cares if we can do something 3% more efficiently, if the right answer is to not do it at all? Or to not produce a product or shut down an office?"

I asked Conde to define SunGard's culture.

"There's no rocket science to this. It's actually very simple—taking pride in doing things the right way, the long way.

"We've had to layoff employees during the downturn, but we've tried to minimize it.

We sacrificed earnings to keep people. The second thing we did was to let go managers, not the workers and programmers. They're the ones who can propel us into the future. The company is very well run and can perform with fewer managers."

Cris summed up by offering suggestions for future business leaders.

"I was very lucky to have parents who told me early on that there were no limits and that I should follow my dreams. I studied astronomy, which is not an obvious means to an end, but you learn more when you study something you love. When people look for jobs they pay too much attention to salary, when that's almost irrelevant when you're starting out. You need to earn enough to live, but it's much more important to make a job choice on the basis of the team you're joining. Over the course of a fulfilling career, you won't remember what you made when you started out."

CEO Think Tank®

ILLUMINATING SOLUTIONS

Congrats on being a winner!

Hope you enjoy the stories — and are inspired to even greater heights!

Warmest regards,
Cheryl Beth Kuchler

HELPING THE FORGOTTEN

DANIEL L. LOMBARDO,
CEO, VOLUNTEERS
OF AMERICA
DELAWARE VALLEY, INC.

"We provide services to people who no one else wants to serve," Dan Lombardo told me. "We help ex-offenders returning to society from the criminal justice system, homeless individuals and families, folks with mental illness and mental retardation, people struggling with domestic violence. We provide senior housing and affordable housing, as well as drug and alcohol treatment.

"Not many traditional service providers will deal with a person who has developmental disabilities," Dan went on, "and who is also aggressive or sexually inappropriate. People who are especially hard to manage are our area of specialty."

Dan runs the Delaware Valley affiliate of the national organization. Based in Collingswood, N.J., its service area is southern New Jersey, Philadelphia and its suburbs, and all of Delaware. Volunteers of America was originally a volunteer movement that split off from the Salvation Army and the name just stuck. The Delaware Valley affiliate has both a professional staff and volunteers, operates 43 separate programs, and serves 12,000 to 15,000 people a year.

Lombardo has been with the Delaware Valley affiliate since August 1988. Only a few months after joining the organization, in March 1989, he took it into Chapter 11.

"We had $3.96 million worth of debt and 399 people on our creditor's list," Dan told me.

"I knew it was bad coming in, but I didn't know how bad. In addition to being a 501(c) for charity, Volunteers of America is also a church. My predecessor was a very prominent collar-wearing minister who was also stealing for Jesus. So it was a very interesting experience. I came in at the request of the national organization.

"I had six months to either make it work or shut it down," Dan went on. "So when I got here, I was on roller skates, going from one thing to another. The sad part is that the organization's credibility was completely gone.

"We had two very fortuitous things happen. We sold a piece of property to the Feds for the expansion of the courthouse in Camden, and a very special woman left us a third of an estate worth $1.6 million. Between the two, we financed the bankruptcy plan and never looked back."

I asked Dan about major milestones he had achieved in the years since.

"We had an 89,000 square-foot train station that was a burned out shell and we had a choice. It was either going to become the largest crack house in North Central Philadelphia, or we were going to do something with it. We pushed the board of directors into developing the building, solicited some HUD dollars, and put together a partnership with an affordable housing developer. We totally renovated the building. We now have 108 units of affordable housing in the building, as well as five social service programs."

Dan's staff is on the front lines, fighting tough battles every day. How does he keep his people motivated and lead them into battle?

"The people who work here bring something to the battle themselves—an abiding commitment to serve. Because if you're in it for the money, you're in the wrong business. We recruit folks who have a sense of mission and purpose in their lives. We spend a tremendous amount of time and energy and money in training them and getting them ready to serve our clients. We provide constant feedback and evaluation to our employees about how they're doing. In addition to that, we've linked performance to salary bonuses, which is something unusual for a not-for-profit. And we provide the best benefits we can."

I was curious if Dan's programs were able meet the demand for social services, especially during the Great Recession.

"We have nine programs in Camden, the second poorest city in the U.S. If it wasn't for us and dozens of other social service providers working there, Camden would be even worse than it is today. The social and human services community is keeping that city together. The demand is always, always much greater than the supply.

"There are two shantytowns in Camden today that no one knows about. As winter comes and the temperature drops, we'll take our vans out and round folks up. If we can get them into the shelter, we have a partnership with Project Hope out of Our Lady of Lourdes Hospital to get them medical attention. Sometimes we feel we're banging our heads against a wall, because public policy doesn't address social problems strategically. If you diverted people away from emergency rooms and invested your charity care costs in community clinics and programs like ours, the money saved would be phenomenal.

"We provide services that should be provided by the government. But because of rules and regulations and a complicated and dehumanizing social services system, people who most need help don't get it."

Dan cited the criminal justice system as another example of failed public policy.

"The United States incarcerates more people than any other country in the world. One out of every 100 people is behind bars. One in 31 is under some form of court supervision.

"Only two states in the country have had a reduction in the prison population, New York and New Jersey, and there's a reason why—because of diversionary programs like ours. According to a recent report, 6,200 inmates in New Jersey could be better served in community-based programs than in the prison system. They're first time offenders. They're low-level drug offenders. What these people need is treatment, not incarceration. For every dollar that you spend on treatment, you save seven dollars in system costs. It's far more effective to spend money on drug rehabilitation than drug incarceration. It just doesn't make any sense. If you moved those 6,200 inmates to community-based programs like the ones we run, you'd save New Jersey taxpayers $166 million a year.

"The Department of Corrections costs $50,000 a year per inmate, and they have a 66% to 85% re-offense rate the first two years in the community. Ex-offenders come to us for $21,000 a year, and we have a 20% re-offense rate. So if we are cheaper and have better outcomes, why aren't you flocking to our doorstep? If we can employ 700 people a year through our programs and get them re-employed as taxpaying members of society, why won't the government give us more money to support and expand that kind of service?"

I asked Dan where his passion for helping others came from. Was he thinking about his life's mission when he was on the playground at age 10?

"My wife recently asked my mother if I'd always been the champion of the oppressed.

My mother said to her, 'Some kids bring home every stray animal. Danny brought home people.' Throughout my career, my primary concern has been people who serve people. I was a foster parent for 16 years. I also worked in state government and worked for a state legislature."

Volunteers of America is a non-profit organization, but it still has to be run like a business. I asked Dan how he balances those two roles.

"The toughest thing in the world is to close programs and services, but sometimes you have no other choice. When the rug is pulled out from underneath you or funding priorities change, what can you do? The reason we've been so stable is because of how we've diversified our base. If we had one or two program lines right now, this would be a very, very tough time. We have a backroom that's really solid and a very talented vice president of finance. We try to keep it focused, because 81 cents of every dollar goes directly to the people that we serve."

It seemed to me that Dan handles the stress very well.

"The more pressure you put on me, the cooler I get. I don't rattle easily. The thing that I really agonize over more than anything else is when funding no longer exists for programs. How do you tell 30 people that they don't have an opportunity to become one of our clients? That's the tough part.

"I remarried about seven years ago, and now I'm down to about 12 or 13 hours a day. It's not as bad as it used to be, because when you're single there are no hours."

How does he unwind?

"I'm a real music junkie. I love to drive my Corvette. And I'm a putzer and a fixer, so every once in a while I get together with the construction and maintenance crew and we'll bang nails. That to me is very therapeutic.

"My Achilles heel is that I try to do too much. For example, there's a population in Camden that we really should be serving. Professional sex workers or prostitutes are a big problem there. A community partner we work with is the only lifeline they have. They don't have any residential services. They don't have any treatment programs. They don't have medical services. And they aren't able to get away from their pimps.

"When I talk to our team about doing this, they ask me how we're going to find the time. They're really grounded, experienced staff, and they keep dragging me back to reality. 'We're already working like rented mules, and you want to add something else?' In other words, don't compromise existing programs by trying to do something new. They keep me very grounded and focused. We're not about titles or structure. We're very, very informal because folks have to feel comfortable enough to tell me that I'm full of it or that I'm pushing them too hard. I think that's one of the things that they value the most. They can cuss and discuss."

To sum up, I asked Dan if we were going in the right direction in helping the poor and underserved in our society.

"One of the rays of hope that President Obama has given us is a sense of compassion and commitment. The problem is that the people who have the use of the media outlets are the most narrow-minded, conservative, and biased people I've ever seen. They use the media to pummel the president. They blame government for our problems, when the only thing that really works to help turn around lives is government and government resources. Look at the attack on the health care plan and all the false rumors that are being laid on this debate. You're talking about vested interests who control the market and don't want to lose that control, even if it means that 50 million people go without healthcare.

"The same thing applies to child welfare in the United States. Why are we number four or five in the world in infant mortality? Why are we number two or three in adolescent pregnancy? If you take a look at Europe, the Scandinavian countries, and Canada, their social systems are far more sophisticated than what we have in this country. Everybody criticizes Canadian healthcare, and yet they have absolutely no understanding of what Canadian healthcare is all about.

"Correctional services in Canada leads the world in intervention strategies for offenders. They've designed programs based on risk and need, and have developed very innovative services. They incarcerate 114 people per 100,000, while we're at 754 per 100,000. It's nuts, absolutely nuts. We're spending billions of dollars for a system that doesn't work, that's locking people up, that's driving California into the poorhouse. If you diverted that money into social service programs, strengthened the family, and supported healthcare, guess what? The amount of money saved would be phenomenal."

FROM THE GROUND UP

KEVIN S. KAN, PRESIDENT AND CEO, AMERICAN AUTO WASH, INC.

When Kevin Kan started with American Auto Wash in September 1999, he decided to learn the business from the ground up.

"The first year I didn't have an official role," he told me, "because I was coming from an executive position in a Fortune 500 company to a family-owned, retail business, something I had no experience with. I wasn't sure if this was a business I would enjoy or whether I wanted to invest in it.

"So I decided to run one of the company's sites, in Coatesville, Pa. I worked there as the manager for six months. I didn't pump gas, because it's self-service, but I worked on the line, washed cars, scrubbed wheels. Before committing myself to the company, I wanted to find out how the business ran and how they made their money. Otherwise, I couldn't effectively run the company."

By washing cars, Kevin learned how the business operated on the most basic levels, an experience that helps him to this day.

"I understand what our managers go through. I understand the difficulties of the hiring process. I understand the difficulties of training and maintaining quality services. When I tell my managers I want things to be done a certain way and they complain, I can say, 'I've been there. I know it's hard, but I know we can do it.' I can speak with authority because I've had the same experience."

From that start, Kan took on more responsibility. He became the de facto president, and in January 2003 acquired a substantial part of the company and assumed the position of CEO.

American Auto Wash, started in 1969 with one combined gas station and car wash, now operates 15 gas stations and 18 full service car washes in Philadelphia and four surrounding counties, employing over 300 people. The company is also a distributor for BP and operates a real estate business. Revenues were about $80 million in 2008.

What does Kan see as the fundamental building blocks of leadership?

"First and foremost, you have to be tough but fair. I have a reputation of being extremely strict, extremely tough. My staff knows that when I say we're meeting at 2 p.m., it means 2:00 and not 2:05 or 2:10. It's very important that your employees understand the standards you want. They have to know exactly what kind of person you are and what you expect of them.

"I don't want to be an employee's buddy or friend. I don't believe that works. I think it confuses your employees, your subordinates. We can have friendly conversations, but first and foremost they're my employees. They all know that, and that's the one thing I know they all know. More than their friend, I want to be the guy that they always want to follow."

Much of Kan's day-to-day work involves monitoring sales numbers.

"When oil prices are shooting up, I lose money because my retail prices cannot cover the rise in my costs. So in a growing market for petroleum, I'm getting killed. Some days I might get an eight or nine cent increase per gallon, and maybe I can raise prices by two cents, if any. If my competition is not moving, I can't move. So I'm sitting there, just eating the loss. The more gallons I sell, the more money I lose. People say, 'Why would you do that?' Because if I raise prices, I'm going to kill my volume. I have to look at the long term also. You have to keep your customers, so that hopefully you make your money back when there's a down market.

"Every morning I look at the reports from 18 retail sites. I can see exactly by location how many gallons we sold, how many car washes we sold, and our margin. I can pick out problems at a site, give them a call, and say, 'Hey, what's happening?' We've also invested in a new state-of-the-art surveillance camera system that lets us visually monitor all the sites. I can wake up on a Sunday morning at home, have my cup of tea, and see at a glance what kind of business we're doing. Are we busy? Is there business coming in?"

Is there a core message or philosophy that Kevin wants people to know about the business?

"When I hire new managers, I always meet with them one-on-one and tell them my philosophy, which is very simple—this is your business. I always say, 'The site that you'll be managing is worth about $2 million to me. So look at it this way—I'm handing over to you a portfolio of mine that's worth $2 million and it's your business. That's how much trust I have in you.'

"You're sure to fail in working for me if you think you're just coming in at 8, leaving at 5, you're not trying to rock the boat, hey, it's not my money. It takes me a week to spot a manager like that.

"We wash about 900,000 cars a year," Kevin went on," and our utility costs per car generally work out to $1. Now, if employees waste water, chemicals, and electricity, that cost goes up by 50 cents per car, which costs me another $450,000 per year. So I need managers who understand that they are accountable and responsible for the company's success or failure. I give them quite a lot of elbow room to decide how they want to market their services."

One way Kan does that is by giving his managers flexibility in deciding how many employees to keep on call and how to schedule them. Managing labor properly is crucial in the car wash business, which fluctuates seasonally and is traditionally much busier in winter months. Kan said he "hit a home run" by instituting a process called "labor benchmarking." The target is to have total labor costs come in at about 30% of gross revenue at each site. Managers are given the flexibility to cut labor, raise revenue by pushing sales, or keep their current labor if they're busy. If they miss the benchmark number, they pay a penalty from their commissions.

"The managers weren't happy with it at the beginning, because part of changing the culture was requiring them to work in an employee position for a minimum of eight hours a week, on the line, as a cashier, or in another role. This has made our labor usage extremely efficient, and we're reaping the benefits of that right now. In 2009, we saw an immediate improvement in our cash flow and profitability."

Kan spent the first 12 years of his life in Hong Kong, where he learned an early lesson about attitude.

"When I was 15, just after 9th grade, I came back to Hong Kong in the summer from boarding school in the U.S., and my father said, 'What are you going to do?'

"I said, 'I don't know, I really haven't thought about it.' He said, 'Well, you have to do something.' I said, 'I'm 15. What job can I get out there?'

"One of my father's best friends owned the entire McDonald's franchise in Hong Kong, and my father said you can work at McDonald's. I come from a very affluent family, and for me to work at McDonalds? I said, 'Are you joking?'

"My father said, 'McDonald's is one of the most successful operations in the world. Go learn something from them.' He called his friend, who said sure.

"When I realized my dad's friend owned all the McDonald's in Hong Kong, I thought, 'Maybe I'll get a pretty good office job in the company headquarters. My dad is good friends with the boss.' So I met him at his office at 9 a.m. that first day, wearing a suit. My dad's friend looked at me and said, 'What are you doing?'

"I said, 'I'm going to work.'

"'In that?'

"I said yeah. He said, 'You're working downstairs in the restaurant.'

"'You're kidding me, right?'

"He said no. So I took off my jacket and tie and put an apron over my white shirt and suit pants. That first day I made Filet-o-Fish. I worked there all summer, and my father picked me up every day from work. When I got in the car, I was reeking of grease and ready to conk out after flipping burgers for eight hours. But my father wanted to talk to me. He'd ask, 'What did you learn today? What differentiates McDonald's from other operations?'

"So I knew after a few days that I would have to pay attention and report to my father every day about what I learned. That's how he raised me. Every generation, we've had leaders come out of our family, and it's very important to us to continue that tradition."

OUTSIDE THE BOX

PETER J. BONI, PRESIDENT AND CEO, SAFEGUARD SCIENTIFICS, INC.

Peter Boni is a decorated combat veteran, having served in the U.S. Army as an infantry officer in Special Operations in Vietnam. He has used this life-altering experience to develop a management philosophy based on the importance of surrounding himself with highly competent, well-trained, and motivated individuals.

"In Vietnam, my number one objective was to see my 25th birthday," he said, "and to make sure my men and I came home alive with all of our arms and legs. When I got home, my next objective was to be vice president of a Fortune 500 company within ten years."

Fast forward to 2010, and Boni has achieved a lot more than that. Peter's background combines both private equity and venture capital experience during his career as a high technology CEO. He has served in executive roles at Fortune 500 companies, and has been a management consultant, board member, investor, and advisor to institutional investors in hardware, software, and technology-enabled services firms.

Today, Boni is president and CEO of Safeguard Scientifics (NYSE: SFE), a holding company that provides capital to entrepreneurs and business professionals in targeted life sciences and technology sectors. These companies have a product or service and want to operate autonomously, but could benefit from additional financing, as well as strategic, operational, and management resources to grow their businesses effectively.

"Our executive and deal teams have domain expertise and operational experience in both the life sciences and technology sectors," Boni told me. "We've been operators ourselves. Beyond just capital, we provide entrepreneurs with the scars on our backs from our own experiences of building businesses and then positioning them to realize a well-timed exit. So as opposed to facing a problem based on some case study we might have read in business school, we have practical experience we can apply.

"My mother was right," Peter went on. "You're judged by the company you keep. I don't like to be a lone ranger. I like friends and family along the way to help me out. So we've developed a significant group of alliances and syndication partnerships with well-known entities, and put together an advisory board. This group is comprised of similarly experienced people with domain expertise in life sciences and technology to help us cultivate our deal flow, qualify it, and ultimately provide some operational assistance to our companies. Our board of directors is composed of similarly experienced individuals in finance, life sciences, and technology."

Safeguard's track record includes Novell, QVC, Cambridge Technology Partners, Internet Capital Group, CompuCom, and Traffic.com.

I asked Peter how Safeguard was different from a venture capital company or a private equity firm.

"There are some similarities to what we do, but we are very different in many arenas. First of all, as far as the investment community is concerned, here you can put in a little bit or a lot. In venture capital or private equity, if you are a limited partner, you also have two choices—you can put in a lot or a lot more. Safeguard provides plenty of liquidity. You can get in or out at any time, as opposed to waiting several years for your first distribution to take place. And we provide the transparency that comes with New York Stock Exchange governance. In addition, we don't play quite as early as the venture capital community, and we don't play quite as late as the private equity community. We are somewhat of an in-betweener. From the entrepreneur's vantage point, there is patience built into our model, and we are never forced to do a premature exit to return capital to limited partners so we can raise a new fund every few years."

Boni went to high school in the Boston area, after attending 11 different schools in several states across the U.S. between the first and ninth grades.

"My father chased defense contracts," he told me. "Little boys have a pecking order, like chickens. Every time when I was the new kid on the block, I had to learn to strike fast. After a while I just got tired of fighting, so I learned how to be charming.

"I'm a working class kid who went to college on my own nickel, with some scholarship money. I played sports and was a leader in various organizations. But the most life altering experience I had was Vietnam.

"I was drafted into the army after college. When I was in officer candidate school, I read that the casualty rates for infantry officers were pretty alarming. I didn't know why at the time, but special operations infantry lieutenants had a statistically meaningful lower casualty rate.

"So I decided to become a special operations infantry officer. You had to apply, get tested, get qualified, and be recommended. I remember my friends and family saying, 'You're going to do what?'

"I said, 'You just have to trust me on this. I'm in a tough spot. I'm trying to give myself the best chance of coming back with all my arms and legs, and my head on straight.'

"So I went off to Vietnam and Cambodia for 15 months in Special Ops, going into remote villages, winning hearts and minds, gathering intelligence about where the bad guys were, and then seeking them out. There are many leadership lessons that I picked up from those adverse circumstances."

I asked Peter to summarize them for me.

"Dig yourself in a foxhole with a team of really good, well-trained people, with whom you share a sense of natural dependence and trust. Collaborate with them. Find people with diverse skills and use a collaborative style, because individually you're just not that good. Have a sense of mission and goal. High-performance decision-making can happen at all levels, if the mission and the goals are well articulated. And no matter what, always move forward.

"Combat is the most stressful, dynamic, and difficult environment," he went on. "You're forced to make decisions—life or death decisions—without having all the information. Sometimes not making a decision is the worst decision you can make, because if you stand still you're certainly going to get shot.

"I later realized that this is why the casualty rates in Special Ops were so much lower. The people were highly trained and extremely motivated, with very specific missions. What I learned was this: if you're not really good, or if I can't train you to be really good, then I don't have room for you in my foxhole. Because either I'm going to get hurt, or I'm going to have to write a letter home about somebody else who got hurt. The lesson was high levels of collaboration with very competent people, and the need for constant communication up and down an organization.

"Without realizing it," Peter concluded, "I took these team building skills and applied them in my business career. I learned to make decisions with incomplete information, evaluate risks, and execute boldly. The Vietnam combat experience gave me pieces of my management style."

I asked Boni how he made the transition from the military to a business career.

"When I got home from Vietnam, my next objective was to be vice president of a Fortune 500 company within ten years. I had been in a management-training program for a big company when I got drafted, and I went back to that company after I got out. I became vice president in eight years, moving from sales and marketing to general management, and then it took another two years to figure out that it was a really lousy job, at least for me.

"Special Ops involved a lot of 'out of the box' thinking, and now I found myself confined to the box. That's why, I believe, some big companies tend to die on the vine. When their business model is challenged by change, they think about yesterday as opposed to tomorrow. I was a tomorrow and forward kind of thinker. The best big company experience I had was as an entrepreneur—starting a division that went from zero to a $100 million in a couple of years."

Boni furthered his career by becoming CEO of generally smaller organizations, ranging from a start-up to a Fortune 1000 firm. At 36, he became CEO of the restart of a fledgling company. It grew to about $50 million, had an IPO, and was acquired by Cisco. Boni also consulted for a while, doing turnaround work for about half a dozen companies. After he sold his last company Peter wanted to do something different, and became an operating partner with a global venture capital and private equity firm in Boston. Boni did mid-market buyouts and early stage technology investing. Then he joined Safeguard Scientifics in 2005.

I asked Boni for his view on recent corporate abuses.

"Stories about the guy who really screwed up or who was overpaid are the things that make the headlines. And that's unfortunate for most CEOs, because that's not the gig they're in.

"You have many constituents as a CEO—your board, your shareholders, your management team, and your customers. You're dealing with competitors, the press, and the outside community. It's an all-encompassing job that can take over your life, if you allow it to.

"I haven't learned how to separate it from my life, so I've integrated it into my personal life, and I think most CEOs will tell you that. But it's not the myth of a fat cat sitting at his desk with his feet up and letting everyone else do the work. The leadership and fiduciary responsibilities involve an awful lot of time and energy.

"I really enjoy what I do," Peter went on. "The advice I gave my children a long time ago is to find your passion in life and then figure out a way to make a living doing that. When you're dead, you're dead a long time, so you better enjoy what you do. Happiness leads to success. It's not the other way around."

Boni breaks down leadership to three principles: focus, vision, and people.

"Have a focus for where you want to go. Then have a clear vision for how to get there. Surround yourself with good, high-quality people. It makes all the difference. Energize them, and get motivation from them as well."

Is there anything keeping him up at night?

"I can't worry about the things where I have no control, and the macro economic climate is something over which I have none. We just need to position ourselves accordingly to the external environment, like water, and adapt to the terrain.

"My mantra is to never be satisfied. The dynamics of the external environment always change. Pop your head up once in a while and check out the changes in the external environment, then alter your positioning based upon what you see."

MAKING TIME TO DREAM

RUDY KARSAN,
CEO, KENEXA

Kenexa provides software solutions, business processes, and expert consulting to help companies with their human resources needs.

"Basically, if you go to Exxon Mobil's website and you hit the career center, we host and manage it for them," Rudy Karsan told me. "If you're working at Time Warner, we manage their annual review process with our software. We run the employee engagement survey for Unilever. So basically anything related to the strategic or human aspects of HR can be outsourced to Kenexa.

"It's about a $5 to $15 billion annual marketplace. We are arguably the largest player in the human capital management field, based on 2008 revenues, among publicly traded companies. We have revenues of over $200 million, with about 1,600 employees in almost 20 countries."

Kenexa was founded in 1987 by Karsan and a co-founder. The company went public in 2005 and is listed on NASDAQ (KNXA). Karsan has been CEO since 1990.

Asked if being a CEO was on his radar as a kid, Karsan said it was "the furthest thing" from his mind. He grew up in Kenya, came to the states via England and Canada, and is an actuary by profession.

I asked Rudy where his leadership skills came from. Sports? Being head of the student council? Being a natural leader as a kid?

"The best way I can answer it is by explaining that the culture in Africa is very different from the culture here in the U.S. I was fortunate that I grew up in an environment where students were ranked in each class. I was usually ranked #1, and that allowed me to take on responsibilities in school. In the old British system you would have prefects and monitors, which don't exist here in the U.S. So by the time I was in grades 5, 6, and 7, I was the head prefect because of my academics. As a result, a lot of kids didn't like me. There's an old British term called 'Being Sent to Coventry,' which means that the rest of the class stops talking to you. I think I held the record for the number of times I was 'Sent to Coventry' by my class."

In addition to academics, Karsan stressed the importance of "helping hands" throughout his career.

"I've been blessed with just incredible, incredible mentors in my life. My third grade teacher took me under his wing and taught me how to build a telescope from scratch. We went down to the field and I looked up to the heavens, and the planets and the moon came a lot closer, and then he showed me Mars. Are you familiar with the term BHAG (Big Hairy Audacious Goal), meaning a great vision? My personal BHAG was set at age nine. I wanted to walk on Mars.

"Mentors have been my guardian angels in two ways. One, they've eliminated obstacles and two, they've given me a swift kick when I needed one. When you go through life, you hit your dark moments. Mentors are there to catch you. I've been blessed with a bunch of catchers, and a lot of those relationships are lifelong relationships."

Karsan built Kenexa from the ground up. I wondered how the company had changed over the years.

"What hasn't changed is our values. This organization is very, very mission oriented.

Let me use an analogy. If Kenexa is an encyclopedia, I'm not the author. I'm simply the person who binds the encyclopedia. My job is to provide enough blank pages for others to write the story. So Kenexa has multiple authors. Everyone who comes in here has the opportunity and freedom to write his or her story. It really isn't my flock. I'm simply the custodian of the flock during this particular period of time. If you notice the business card, there is no title on it. So there's always this notion of partnership."

Karsan was optimistic about the company's future.

"From a purely revenue perspective, our growth has historically been 60% organic and 40% acquisitive. If I look into the future, I see a lot of growth. Our BHAG for the company is to get to $1 billion in revenue by 2015. Last year, we touched the lives of 100 million people through our systems."

When asked about key mistakes he had made and what he had learned from them, Karsan was disarmingly frank.

"There's a whole history of them. My lack of understanding of cash has almost taken the company under three or four times. That cash is king is a lesson that I've probably learned more than three or four times, and I wish I had learned it the first time.

"The other kind of mistake that I've made over and over again is making judgment calls on people. I tend to be a little rash on that, so I tend to give up on people fairly quickly. Then there's no way for them to redeem themselves, and when I look back after two years I can see that I really screwed up there. I lost a really good person because of my own stubbornness.

"Fundamentally, most of my errors are the result of ego. When I either want my name in lights or applause at a certain point, that's when I end up making flawed decisions. Ego is a nasty thing because it's really driven by insecurities. Essentially, I'm still that foreigner who's trying to hustle, and at times I've let my fear and ego drive a lot of decisions. When I look back, I can say to myself, 'You didn't do it for the benefit of the company, the clients, or the employees, and now you're paying the price.'"

I asked Karsan how he apportions his time in a typical day.

"I always have trouble answering this question because as a CEO you have to discriminate between time spent doing and time spent thinking. If I look at 'doing time,' I probably spend about 40% to 50% of my time either outside of Philadelphia or outside the country, meeting with employees, customers, and investors. In my mind, CEO stands for our three most important stakeholders—our clients, our employees and our owners. So I look at serving those three stakeholder groups."

Karsan describes his "thinking" time as equally crucial to his work.

"I don't know how to put this well, but I dream a lot. Dreaming has a negative connotation in our language today. People will say, 'He's a dreamer' or 'She'll never get anything done because all she has is dreams.' But to me, dreaming is the single biggest gift we're given by our creator, no matter how you wish to define that. It's the one thing you can do if you're in the bowels of this planet or in the deepest jail. It can never be taken away from you. It's not conscious, it's not planned, it just kind of happens, and I never curtail the dreaming, because it's a gift.

"I also engage in serious meditation, prayer, and introspection. It's daily, 30 to 60 minutes a day. It's fairly regimented. I'll never shortchange my meditation time, my dreaming time, or my praying time."

I asked Karsan about public perceptions of CEOs as greedy and corrupt.

"Business leadership in this country has been seriously lacking for the last ten years. Some people have been caught with their hands in the cookie jar, and it's not just the odd rotten apple. The level of fraud is so mind-boggling and the greed is so high that I don't really blame the newspapers. I completely understand the general American perception of their business leaders and I don't disagree with them. There haven't been a few isolated cases of fraud, but multiple scenarios associated with tremendous levels of criminal activity. It's hard for me to turn around and say the media is wrong.

"Having said all that, I do believe with most of the CEOs I know personally are, on the whole, caring people, and their success has generally been the result of some form of service rather than some form of self-centeredness."

Rudy spends about 500 to 1,000 hours a year in not-for-profit work, particularly in projects related to international development in Central Asia, India and Pakistan, and Africa. In 2007, he did fieldwork in hospitals in Afghanistan and education work in Mumbai, India.

To sum up, I asked Karsan about the importance of human capital management in today's business world.

"We have data that show you can predict your future financial outcomes based on the degree to which your employees are engaged in their work. The problem is that workers are often treated in ways that can be seen as ruthless or devoid of any emotion. To a certain extent I understand it, because the only reason the corporation exists is for profit. That's by definition what a corporation is. And the corporation can be brutal, just like nature is brutal. Nature is very kind to the species, very brutal to the individual member. The business world is very kind to businesses, brutal to the individual company. Organizations are very kind to their employees as a whole, but very often brutal to individual members of the organization.

"Somehow, organizations need to figure out how to establish and nurture the best possible relationships with their workers, and that's what our business tries to help them do."

EVERY BUSINESS IS A PEOPLE BUSINESS

DAVID BINSWANGER, PRESIDENT AND CEO, BINSWANGER

Binswanger is a third-generation family owned business, founded by David's grandfather Frank G. Binswanger, Sr. during the height of the Depression in the early 1930s.

Family businesses that make it into the third generation are unusual, with the odds (and statistics) working against that happening. David pointed out that in any business there will be disagreements, but "if you put the family first, you'll resolve your differences."

"We can get in a room, fight about an issue for an hour, but then figure out what to do," he told me. "That's because we're able to create a common vision together. When you understand that family is more important than the business, you figure out ways to make sure that you're on the same page, even when your personalities are different or when you're not necessarily agreeing at the end of the day."

Headquartered in Philadelphia, Binswanger specializes in real estate services for mid to large sized companies around the world. Its clients include ExxonMobil, Comcast, General Motors, Wal-Mart, Intel, and many others. Binswanger helps them buy, sell, build, finance, and value real estate—everything from a small sales office to a large chip manufacturing plant in the middle of Costa Rica.

Over the years, Binswanger has grown from a single Philadelphia office to an international real estate leader with offices on five continents. David's grandfather made that growth possible by anticipating trends and seizing opportunities, particularly in the Sunbelt.

"He was an entrepreneur who opened an office in 1956 in Charlotte, North Carolina," David said, "which is the first time a real estate company ventured out of its local area. That got us to focus on major corporations and major institutional moves, which is how the company expanded nationally in the 60s and 70s, and then internationally in the 80s and 90s."

David gave the Comcast Center in Philadelphia as an example of a recent successful project.

"We were not the developer, but we were involved in creating and negotiating the deal. The developer delivered the building as a shell, and we were responsible for the interior. The Comcast Center is now a landmark in Philadelphia."

Although he grew up in a business family, David felt little pressure as a child to follow that career route.

"My father encouraged us to figure out what we wanted to do on our own," he said. "When I graduated from college, I decided I didn't want to be in the business."

After attending Bowdoin College in Maine, David worked for IBM for a couple of years as a systems engineer, designing software packages for large insurance companies. He then earned an MBA at Harvard Business School and decided to join the family business.

"They started me literally on the street," David said. "I had done a summer or two in the management offices, so I had been involved in the day to day management of an office building. They had me knock on doors. I wasn't handed the reins."

In the mid 1990s, David started taking on more of a management role, and he became CEO in 1998.

I asked David what advice he would give to aspiring CEOs. He mentioned the importance of understanding your strengths and weaknesses, "so you can take advantage of your strengths and figure out how to get around your weaknesses." But then he put the role of CEO in a broader perspective.

"If you put work first, you're making a huge mistake. If family and community, no matter how you define them, are not equally important to you and part of your life, you're probably not going to be a great leader. You may understand the numbers, but you'll never understand the people. Every business is a people business, no matter what it is. When you lose track of that, you're in trouble. The financial crisis, in my opinion, was the result of putting numbers before people."

While criticizing recent corporate abuses, David also pointed out the difficulties inherent in leading a large company.

"People expect you, as a leader, to always be out in front and know where you're going, when that's not always the case," he said. "I compare it to being the captain of an oil tanker in the fog. Your visibility isn't great. You may not have the time to stop and turn the ship around. You're always trying to guess, and if you miscalculate you run up on the shore and have a major oil spill.

"We tend to judge people not by what they knew at the time they made a decision, but by what happened at the end. If you're successful, even as the result of a bad decision, you get the credit. But if you're not successful, even when you made the right decision or did the best you could at the time, you're considered a failure. I don't think that's necessarily fair.

"A family business puts us in a different kind of responsibility," he went on. "We don't have to report to anybody, so we really have to make decisions based on our values. We like to think of our employees as an extended family. That doesn't mean that everybody is going to be treated like they're my brother or my son, but it does mean we can reach out, be understanding, and show compassion when someone is having a problem."

I asked David what he would like his legacy to be.

"That I've contributed to the community and impacted some people's lives for the good. I always tease people that I want a Quaker funeral even though I'm Jewish. I love the Quaker funeral because instead of having one or two people eulogize, anyone who wants to may get up to say something. It demonstrates how many different ways one person has touched other people's lives."

David has a prosthesis in place of his right arm. I wasn't sure whether to bring it up, but then he mentioned he was willing to talk about it. I asked him the obvious question: was the injury a defining moment in his life?

"I'm going to give you a different answer from what you might be expecting," he replied. "But first I'll tell you what happened.

"I was on a trip in the Galapagos Islands. I had an underwater camera and was in the water taking pictures of sharks and turtles for my kids. It was the most ideal setting you could imagine. And then a boat ran over me and severed my arm.

"I always describe it as the best day of my life. I had an epiphany—not a word I use lightly—that the arm saved my life. When the boat ran over me, it came within a centimeter of my spine. Had that happened, I would have drowned.

"Mentally, it's an easy trade to make if somebody asks you, 'Would you cut off your arm to save your life?' I didn't make that decision, but that's what happened. The fact that we stopped the bleeding, the fact that I stayed alive through the 20 hours it took to get me out, and the fact that the arm blocked the boat from taking out my spine made it the best day of my life.

"I was very quickly able to get a prosthetic that moves when I think and that looks real. I wouldn't say I didn't struggle with it, but I didn't have as difficult a time in dealing with my body. The experience also gave me the opportunity to have conversations with people that I would never have had, about what's important to them and how special they are, and that's a gift.

"Having said all that, I'm very proud that I don't feel it was the defining moment of my life. My priorities and my outlook were in good shape before the accident, so I didn't need to readjust them. People were important to me before I lost the arm, and they were important to me after.

"The main thing I learned is that you can look at any situation, whether business or personal, from a lot of different angles. Obviously, being run over by a boat can be considered the worst day in your life. But you can also turn it around and walk to the other side and say, 'No, it's not. It's the best day.' And as soon as you believe it, you have totally changed the outcome.

"You have the ability to view any situation in a way that can help you move forward in life. That doesn't mean you should always be happy about the things that happen to you, but you have the ability to control how you see them and use them. And that's a big deal."

MONEY IS THE REWARD, NOT THE REASON

ED SNIDER,
CHAIRMAN,
COMCAST-SPECTACOR

From a very early age, Ed Snider was interested in business.

"I can't say it's true for everyone," Ed told me, "but I feel a large percentage of entrepreneurs are born that way. Remember how you had friends in school who always knew they wanted to be doctors or lawyers? I never gave a second thought to wanting to be a doctor, but I was always looking to do things related to business."

Snider was fortunate to have a father who encouraged his interests.

"My father had a little grocery store in D.C. when I was a kid," he went on. "Dad was fantastic. Even when I was eight years old he let me rearrange the shelves. He let me use my own mind. He wasn't the kind of father to say, 'No, you can't do that.' He just had phenomenal instincts on how to raise his son. In raising my own children, I still use 90% of the stuff I learned from him."

Today, Snider is chairman of Comcast-Spectacor, the Philadelphia-based sports and entertainment firm.

"We own the Philadelphia Flyers, the Philadelphia 76ers, the Wachovia Center and Wachovia Spectrum," Ed explained. "We own Comcast SportsNet Philadelphia, a regional 24-hour sports programming network. We have a ticketing company, New Era Tickets, a food concession company, Ovations Food Services, and an international management company, Global

Spectrum. We manage arenas, stadiums, convention centers throughout the country and in Canada, and we're now expanding throughout the world."

Of all his numerous achievements in business, Snider is perhaps most proud of his role in bringing the Flyers to Philadelphia in 1967 as an expansion team. The league was doubling from six to 12 teams that year, but Philadelphia was not on most people's radar for a team. Snider waged a one-person campaign to convince the NHL otherwise.

"I think my biggest achievement was creating the Flyers out of thin air where everybody said it was going to fail," he said. "Hockey in Philadelphia? Nobody even knew what a puck was. There had been an NHL team in Philly in the 1930s that had the worst record in the league, drew no fans, and lasted one year. So when I wanted to bring major league hockey to the city, everybody thought I was nuts. The *Hockey News* voted us the least likely to succeed of the six expansion teams. But I was young enough to be nuts.

"The reason I ended up with as much of the team as I did is because I had tremendous difficulty getting financing. I wanted to own 10% of the team and get a bunch of investors. I originally owned 60% and eventually ended up owning 90%.

"But I was young enough to be confident that we could make it work. As it turned out, of the six original expansion teams that came into the league, we're probably the only one that has been consistently successful. It's been a gigantic success."

The new team needed an arena. Snider convinced city officials that he would build one, if they would provide him five acres of land on what was supposed to be part of the parking lot for the new Veterans Stadium. Snider oversaw the construction of the Spectrum and eventually took control of it.

Snider attends 76ers and Flyers games to keep in touch with how well the company is performing. "Being at the games tells me a lot about our operation," he said. "Not only the team on the court, but what's going on in the stands, how we're treating the fans, and all the other things that are involved in the hospitality business."

But Snider also pointed out how his management style has evolved over the years.

"When you're starting something and you have to make it work or you're broke, you're a micromanager. You know every single detail of every single thing that's going on. So when I started the Flyers and the Spectrum, I knew absolutely everything that was going on because I had to make payroll every week and I didn't know how I was going to do it. Now that we've grown and are much more prosperous, I don't micromanage. My people keep me informed and the things that come my way are the things that are really important. I put someone in a job and let them do it."

Ed is particularly proud of his Ed Snider Youth Hockey Foundation, which he founded to help youth in inner city Philadelphia.

"I grew up in some tough, anti-Semitic neighborhoods. I got into a lot of fights. I never started a fight, but I had to learn to fight to defend myself. It toughened me up. Fighting with your fists is one thing, but kids who fight today might blow someone away with a gun and think nothing of it.

"I'm particularly concerned about Hispanic, black, and some white kids in the inner city in Philadelphia. I always wanted to do something for them but I didn't know exactly what. Finally, through discussions with people in the organization, I decided to focus on hockey as a way to help these kids. Not to create hockey stars, but to teach them life skills. Through our foundation, they learn what teamwork is. We teach them how to shake hands and how to look people in the eye, all the life skills that are neglected for these kids. And the satisfaction that I get from this is unbelievable."

The Foundation now operates in five city rinks, serving 2,500 kids, both boys and girls. To enroll, young people have to maintain good grades and attendance in school.

"Our goal is to serve 10,000 kids," Ed said. "Every dollar that someone contributes to the Foundation, I put in two. We spend a couple million dollars a year.

"We get letters from the mothers about how the program saved their children's lives. One girl wrote a letter that brought tears to my eyes. She said she never thought she had any chance in life, but now she feels optimistic because she's no longer on the streets."

I concluded by asking Ed his advice for aspiring CEOs.

"I think you have to really love what you do and believe in what you're doing. And you have to be honest. Totally 100% honest. Let's say that you and I are making a deal. I'll be 100% honest with you. Not 99%, but 100%. I'll tell you exactly what I want. A lot of people in business think they have to be shrewd and play angles. I can't tell you how many times people have left a meeting with me wondering, 'What's his angle?'

"I didn't have an angle. My father told me if you never tell a lie, you don't have to remember what you said. I've always lived by that. I may not say everything that's on my mind. Obviously, nobody can. But I don't lie, and that disarms people.

"And my other mantra is, 'Money is the reward, not the reason.' I've never run these businesses on the basis of the bottom line having to go up 10% each year. I don't believe in that. I couldn't run a public company. You have to make decisions for the bottom line and not for the right reasons. Can you imagine running a sports team and saying you have to cut your best player because the bottom line has to go up 10%?

"I don't run any organization that way because it's not the money that's the prime motivation. It's the satisfaction of doing something well and succeeding at it. The money is the reward. I never thought I'd have what I have today. It wasn't even a goal. I knew guys who had the goal of becoming a millionaire by age 30. The only goal I had was to feed my family. This wasn't a goal. This just happened."

NURTURING A CULTURE OF VALUES

HOWARD B. STOECKEL, PRESIDENT AND CEO, WAWA, INC.

Howard Stoeckel, President and CEO of Wawa, is deeply passionate about the company's value system.

"People wonder, how do you make decisions? They're curious about what people do when they sit in a room. I say it's not as difficult as you think, because when you have a well-defined value system it makes decision making very easy.

"We have six deeply held values that guide almost everything we do in this business. Value people. Delight customers. Do things right. Do the right things. Embrace change. Have a passion for winning. If decisions embrace most of those values, they prove to be very, very successful decisions."

Headquartered in the Pennsylvania town of the same name, Wawa has been in business for 200 years. It started out as a manufacturing firm in Millville, N.J., and it's evolved over that period into a convenience retailer that sells food, gas, and convenience store goods on one piece of property. (Wawa is the Native American word for the Canada Goose, found throughout the Delaware Valley.) The privately-owned company operates 570 stores in Virginia, Maryland, Pennsylvania, New Jersey, and Delaware, and employs about 17,000 people.

At the core of the company's value system, Howard told me, is the relationship with individual customers.

"People identify with their local Wawa store. That's the magic that makes this business whole. My most important role is to nurture and manifest that culture, and to protect and nurture those relationships.

"This is a difficult business. It's one customer at a time, one transaction at a time, and it all comes down to that relationship with the people. Our stores tend to be places where you're known by name. A place where you have a fun and friendly experience, even if only for a few minutes each day. Where you see familiar faces, and if you want to stay and talk a little bit and socialize, you're welcome to do so.

"That's what separates us from our competitors. We don't desire to dot the landscape of this country, east to west, north to south. We want to be the best we can be.

"So we put heavy emphasis on what happens in the stores. This is not a hierarchical organization, but rather a bottom up type of organization. We like to empower our people in the stores. Our general managers are all promoted from within. They grow up here. They live the value system. They work hard for the value system. We hire for values and we promote for the values."

Stoeckel has been with Wawa for 23 years and in 2004 became the first person outside the founding family to become CEO. I asked Howard if becoming a CEO had always been his goal.

"I was working at Wanamaker's in 1967 when they just hired a new CEO. The employees went to an auditorium, where he introduced himself and talked about his vision for the business. I was about 22 at the time, and I could remember saying to myself, 'Boy, that would be a great opportunity, to be able to run the business.'

"Did I set myself on that goal? No. Throughout my career, I've made it a point to have jobs that I loved, and if I didn't love the job, I moved on. I let my passions guide my actions. If I became a CEO that would be great, but I wanted to do the best I could at whatever I was doing at the time.

"My greatest satisfaction has been watching other people grow. I think that's why I'm sitting here today. When I look back at achievements, I don't remember the numbers as much as I do the people that I've worked with over four decades. I really think leadership is all about helping other people dream. It's about helping other people achieve their goals, because as you work your way up in an organization, you realize how dependent you are on everyone else. It's all about getting the right people in the right positions and making sure they feel good about what they're doing."

Wawa's employees own 28% of the company, with 8,000 out of 17,000 associates participating in an employee stock ownership program.

"So I wake up each morning and think about how I work for them," Howard told me. "The value of this company is going to determine their well being in the decades to come, their retirement, their ability to put kids through college. That's where I have to set my priorities and what I have to protect and nurture. I'm not working for shareholders who are institutional investors. I'm not working for Wall Street analysts. The people that I'm working for are right here—the 8,000 people who are part of the Wawa team, just like I am."

Like many CEOs I spoke with, Howard emphasized that his company's culture is tied to being privately held.

"We do the right things long term because we don't have Wall Street pressure. This is not a quarter-by-quarter business. In this business, with gas prices so volatile, you can't predict quarters anyway. From a profit standpoint, you can have a pleasant surprise or a big disappointment because there's no way of predicting what's going to happen with field margins. Prices just go up and down, and sometimes there's no logic, rhyme, or reason with fuel prices."

I asked Howard how he blows off steam and manages stress.

"First, I enjoy my job. It's like a hobby. If you enjoy your work, and if you're in alignment with your role and responsibilities, it reduces the stress load. I always had stress in my career when I wasn't as compatible with the organization or my job.

"Also, I'm not a workaholic. Do I wake up seven days a week and think about what needs to be done and the people of Wawa? I do. But I get away from it through travel, vacations, and a change of scenery. Balance is important. I've gotten some of my best ideas not in the office, but when I've been to places where I can begin to clear my head."

When I asked about mentors, Howard said he learns "from everyone."

"Just because you've been successful, it doesn't mean you're going to continue to be successful. You really have to understand what makes you successful and then make sure you protect it and reinvest in it.

"I'll talk to people here at all levels of the business. I'll use my wife as a sounding board. She likes to travel the stores and she knows a lot of people. Yesterday, for Thanksgiving, she took cookies out to eight stores, and she gets the pulse of the organization. So she gives me a lot of insight."

Howard has a giant yellow crayon in his office, about four feet tall, not a typical sight in most corporate offices.

"I've had this crayon with me for over two decades now. It's here to remind people to think big, have fun, and stay young. Businesses that grow old die before their time, and businesses that succeed are youthful and stay young."

FINDING A NICHE

IRVIN E. RICHTER,
CHAIRMAN AND CEO,
HILL INTERNATIONAL, INC.

Irv Richter started Hill International in his house in February 1976.

"I took one son," Irv told me, "moved him into the other son's bedroom, and used the spare bedroom as my office."

From that modest start, Hill International, headquartered in Marlton, N.J., has grown into one of the largest construction claims and management firms in the world, with 2,300 employees in 80 offices worldwide. The company helps clients minimize the risks inherent in the construction process by supporting every phase of a project, from planning and design, to procurement and construction, to start-up and operation.

Irv's story shows the power of initiative and taking the right risks. Before he founded Hill, he was working for a small company of about 10 employees, which specialized in developing computerized scheduling programs for contractors, to help keep their projects on track.

"The first day I got there, they had gotten a call from a client the day before," Irv told me. "The guy I'm working for tells me we have a problem, let's go out and see the contractor about it. I said, 'What's the problem?' He said he has a claim. I said, 'What's the claim?' He says, 'We've never done one, so let's go talk to him about his issues.'"

Richter explained what a construction claim entails.

"A claim occurs when a construction project gets delayed and costs you more money than originally planned. Sometimes unanticipated conditions cause problems. How come the ground was softer than expected? How come there was rock or water where none was expected? You get into these disputes and if it costs the contractor more money, he's going to look to recover it through a change order, which the owner can accept or reject. A claim is a rejected change order request. You've got to prove that the claim cost you money and that you're entitled to be compensated for it.

"Since this company had never done a claim before," Irv went on, "the owner figured he might as well give it to me, the new guy on the block. I didn't know that much about construction. My limited experience was with gym floors, squash courts, and racquetball courts. My previous employer manufactured these courts, and when the floors would get wet and buckle, I resolved the disputes over whose fault it was."

In a project for a sewage treatment agency, the contractor had problems with concrete passing hardness tests, which delayed construction almost a year. Irv set out to determine what caused the delay and whether the contractor had the ability to recover.

"The contractor did everything he could and the concrete still wasn't passing," Irv told me. "What he didn't know was that the superintendent of the construction company was having an affair with the wife of the inspection company's president. The concrete was never going to pass, and the aggravation almost put the contractor into a mental institution. The project was delayed until the following spring."

Although he had never done a claim before, Richter went to work. "I assumed that the contractor's lawyer would know no more about construction than I did," Irv said, "and I knew nothing. I knew about gym flooring, but that was about all."

Richter wrote a chronology of what happened over a period of several weeks, described the meetings between the owner, contractor, and architect, and footnoted everything with supporting documents. He went to a bookstore and bought construction and engineering dictionaries, and drew illustrations of technical problems that he added to the report. Irv laid out all the problems in his report and calculated that the contractor had a $500,000 claim.

"I got the report to the lawyer on a Friday. Monday morning he calls me up and says, 'Irv, I finally understand what the contractor was trying to tell me. I never understood it before. You made it as clear as could be. I've got another client who has a problem like this. Can you represent him too?'"

From that point, the company's claim business started to take off.

"When I first joined the company, they were doing $25,000 a month. When I left the company, they were doing $125,000 a month and I was doing $100,000 in claims a month. I would hire experts, pay them a certain amount, and convert what they said into English, from technical into layman's language."

Richter found he had a natural ability to do construction claims.

"I can't tell you why. I can't explain why someone walks down the street, a tune comes into his head, and he writes a hit song. I just had the ability to see my way very clearly through these problems. They would say to me, 'That's exactly what happened on the job. How did you know?' I just seemed to know what had happened."

Irv then decided to strike out on his own and form his own construction claims company.

"I didn't look at it as risk taking. I didn't form Hill as an entrepreneur looking to take a risk, because I don't think most entrepreneurs are risk takers. That's why most entrepreneurs tend to be groups, not individuals. To the contrary, most entrepreneurs are risk avoiders. One of the reasons they start a business is they're convinced that if they don't do so, they're going to lose their jobs. That was true in my case. I was convinced that the guy I was working for was going to kill the business. And he tried to do just that when I enrolled in law school at night. He told me to quit law school or he would fire me after the first semester. So I started Hill. I later went back, finished law school, and became a member of the bar, licensed to practice all the way up to the Supreme Court."

Irv's first case with his own company involved a sewer line that had flooded and killed some people, causing a delay.

"This was a project on which the contractor was hoping to recover $400,000. We settled for $1 million on the claim. The opposing lawyer held up my report in the arbitration. He said, 'Irv, I want you to know this is the reason we're settling.' I couldn't believe he said that, so I brought my client into the room and asked him to repeat what he said and he did.

"What I found during my investigation was that they knew they had a real problem with flooding, but never gave the contractor that information. We found the smoking gun. Sometimes there really is a smoking gun."

As Irv's company got more and more projects, he was invited to speak at seminars on construction claims. His first seminar drew 400 people in New York City. His company was gaining momentum.

"By November I knew I needed a secretary, and I was trying to figure out whether to put her in the living room, the kitchen, or the dining room. Time to get an office, and then I started hiring people. That's when I realized that we were going to stay in business for a while. We had a 900 square-foot office and within six months we outgrew it."

Irv said one of the keys to his success was finding a niche and exploiting it.

"One way to grow a business is to do more of the same, and the other way is to open up a new area. We started in a very, very small area. We were the first firm to go into construction claims as a business, not as a sideline. It made sense to me that if you hired us at the beginning of a project and not at the end, we could help you avoid the things that go wrong, because we knew everything that could go wrong on a job."

Irv stressed the importance of communication skills in his business. Many engineers he hired had the technical expertise, but not the necessary communication skills for the job.

"When I started the company, I had engineers who couldn't string two sentences together and know there was a period in between. I rewrote a lot of the claim documents myself. You have to be able to communicate. You have to convince. In a lot of ways it was a sales pitch you were making to the owner, that the contractor was entitled to this money. So it had to be convincing, well written, and supported by the facts. If you're making a lot of mistakes and you're sloppy, the owner is going to figure you'll be sloppy in your testimony. You have to convince them to settle it and not go to court."

In concluding, Irv distinguished between having a vision and being able to manage people effectively.

"The most critical thing in running a business is being able to deal with people," he said. "The other is having vision. Those skills don't necessarily overlap. Having a vision often has nothing to do with your ability to deal with people. That's why I believe most entrepreneurs are generally very limited in being able to run a big business. They don't delegate. They don't bring in a management team. They want to do everything themselves. The growth of these kinds of companies tends to flatten out. Whether they grow or not depends on whether they bring in high quality, capable management. This is a critical, critical issue in growing and managing a business."

A BUSINESS WITH A HEART

JAY SPECTOR,
CEO,
JEVS HUMAN SERVICES

Jewish Employment and Vocational Service (JEVS) was founded in 1941 by a group of concerned citizens to help Jewish refugees from Europe make a successful transition to life in Philadelphia.

"They helped refugees with employment and language training, to get people into that first job and on the road to success in our community," said Jay Spector, the organization's CEO.

Eventually JEVS evolved beyond assisting just the Jewish community to serving very diverse groups throughout the larger Philadelphia community, including individuals with physical, developmental, and emotional challenges, senior citizens, the unemployed, people on public assistance, and individuals in the corrections system.

Today, JEVS Human Services is one of the largest private nonprofit organizations in the Delaware Valley, serving close to 20,000 people each year, with an annual budget of nearly $90 million and over 900 employees.

The organization's fastest growing program provides personal care to people who are aging or disabled in their own homes.

"These are people who otherwise would have to go to a nursing home," Jay told me. "We're able to bring in about 30 hours of care a week, and that can make the difference between a family sending their loved one to a nursing home or staying at home. Most families would rather let their loved ones stay at home as long as possible. People just need some help, and it's not round the clock help that they need."

That program now serves 4,000 people, up from 800 in the last five years. JEVS has expanded the program throughout 44 counties in Pennsylvania, as well as in New Jersey and Delaware.

When state institutions for people with mental retardation were being closed down because of neglectful care, the state and the city approached JEVS about opening group homes. The organization now serves 120 mentally disabled clients in over 30 group homes.

JEVS also serves about 1,500 individuals at Orleans Technical Institute, which provides intensive employment training in a wide variety fields, including the building trades, court reporting, and human services.

"We've worked with over 1,000 inmates in the Philadelphia prison system, helping them learn a trade, so when they come out they have an extra step in not returning to a life of crime," Jay explained. "We've been working aggressively with the city to figure out how to lower the recidivism rate. One approach is to start working with someone while he or she is incarcerated, and follow through with a plan and resources that help that individual transition into the community."

A native Philadelphian, Spector earned a graduate degree in urban and regional planning and started his professional career as a manpower employment and training planner for the City of Philadelphia. He became director of planning, which helped him become familiar with the non-profit sector. Spector then joined JEVS in 1979.

"I had opportunities to lead other organizations, not just be the number two, but I came to JEVS because it was not a single purpose agency. Its diversity was a great strength. They had employment training programs, but they also did mental health and mental retardation, substance abuse, and had a social entrepreneur model. I figured, as a young guy, I could learn all these fields and become an expert in not just one area but in many." Spector become CEO in 1995.

Spector describes JEVS as a "hybrid between a business and a non-profit. We have an expression we use—we're a business with a heart.

"Today, the non-profit world is more like the for-profit world," he went on. "There's a whole new sense of risk in the non-profit world and it's changed the way you run your organization. You have to make sure you understand data, how to bill, and how to use sophisticated technology resources. You need to understand what it costs to deliver a unit of service. You have to find a way of building in those costs, otherwise you're going to die. You have to have good solid business practices. You need to know and understand what performance means and how to live within a budget.

"We've moved away from just getting government grants, paying salaries, and hoping that things turned out well. Now everything we do is either fee for service or a performance-based payment contract."

Jay described his management style as "deliberate."

"Every decision has to be thought through strategically. Sometimes when you rush to make a decision, you fail to consider all the possible ramifications."

He makes it a point to visit each of the organization's 40 programs once a year.

"We're getting more dispersed geographically, and it becomes hard to get out and see every program. If there's anything that I miss from when we were smaller, it's that.

"But you want your employees to know that you care about them and that there's somebody behind them. So I spend a lot of time doing town meetings with each business unit or program that we operate.

"I'll spend a couple of hours sharing some of the trends that could affect their lives or the people we're serving. I'll ask for their input, I'll share what I'm proud of, and I expect them to share what they're proud of. I let them brag and feel good about themselves because they do hard work. They need to take time to honor themselves. So we'll have an exchange and use that information to strengthen our organization, strengthen programs, and change processes. It's all good intelligence collecting."

For the future, Spector is concerned with how JEVS sustains itself over the long term.

"I want to become less dependent on the federal government, state government, local government. Part of that vision is to try to create some kind of endowed fund at JEVS to pay for some of our services over the long haul. For example, it would be great thing if our students at the Orleans Center could come to school without having to take out heavy loans."

The other challenge, he said, is how to market the organization's core services to a broader area, without giving up anything it's doing in the Philadelphia marketplace.

Spector finds it important to gain an objective, outside perspective on the challenges he faces.

"The person at the top of an organization can have difficulty finding somebody to talk to openly and objectively. I deal with that through an executive coach, who I meet with once or twice a month. She keeps me on top of new information and trends. She'll identify things that I should read, versus the ten million things I'd love to find time to read. She's been very helpful around professional development, to make sure our people get what they need to do their jobs. I also belong to several trade associations where I can talk to peers in my field, compare notes, and commiserate."

Jay finds balance through the satisfaction of his work.

"Computers and technology have made it very difficult to walk away from work. You can be on the top of Machu Picchu and looking at your damn emails. But I make sure that I have a life of balance. Even though I may be working longer and harder than ever, it's a labor of love. I don't let the stresses get to me. I just enjoy being part of a creative, problem solving organization. It keeps my juices going. As long as I can continue to do that, this job will never be a burden to me."

OWN WHAT YOU DO

JOSEPH CORADINO, PRESIDENT, PENNSYLVANIA REAL ESTATE INVESTMENT TRUST (PREIT)

When I walked into the office of Pennsylvania Real Estate Investment Trust, I knew I was among Philadelphians. On one wall there's a painting of the El at 46th and Market. In Joe Coradino's office, there's a painting of the Italian Market in South Philly.

"We're all local people," Joe told me.

PREIT, founded in 1960 and one of the first equity REITs in the U.S., invests primarily in retail shopping malls and community centers. The company's current portfolio consists of 54 retail properties, including over 40 shopping malls and 13 community centers. The company has properties in 13 states, primarily in the mid-Atlantic region, and employs 700 people.

Headquartered in Philadelphia, PREIT merged with The Rubin Organization, a commercial property development and management firm, in 1997. Joe is the President of PREIT services, which is likened to a Chief Operating Officer, while Ronald Rubin is Chairman and CEO.

"We've been on a run," Joe told me. "In 1997, the company had a market cap just under $400 million, and we built that to a $4 billion market cap. We bought all of the Rouse Company's assets in the Philadelphia market, and then we bought a publicly traded, family run company, Crown American, based in Johnstown, Pa. We had 12 properties, they had 32. We acquired that company, integrated its employees and management teams, and made it work. So we built PREIT dramatically, from eight malls to 40, and the ball started rolling down a hill at that point."

Joe spends much of his day overseeing the process of securing tenants, which he calls "the heart and soul of the business."

"I focus a good deal of my time on making sure the transactional process works as smoothly and as quickly as possible. It starts with identifying a prospective tenant, establishing a relationship with that tenant, then moving from a proposal to a letter of intent, and then to a lease. And then to construction plans, construction, and the opening.

"Lots of different people and disciplines touch that process—sales people, architects, attorneys, engineers, contractors, and property managers. The tighter you can get that process, the quicker you can move from prospect to tenant."

Joe grew up in South Philadelphia, served in the Army, and then put himself through Temple University and graduate school at the University of Arizona, where he earned a degree in city planning.

"I learned about the shopping center business from a gentleman out there by the name of Roy Drachman. Roy got me my first job. I went to work for Morris Kravitz at Kravitz Properties in Philadelphia and he really taught me the business. He was a fabulous mentor for me. He taught me some of my greatest lessons.

"I remember the first week or so on the job, I was walking through a mall with Mr. Kravitz and I passed by a piece of litter on the floor. Mr. Kravitz stopped, leaned over to pick it up, and said, 'Joseph, would you walk by that in your home?' And I got it.

"Another day he came into my office, sat down in the chair in front of me, and said, 'Joseph, if you don't get a deal done, or if you don't get a lease done because the secretary couldn't type the lease or the lawyer was on vacation or the Federal Express guy came late, do you know whose fault it is? It's your fault. Take responsibility. Own what you do.' If you own what you do, if you take pride in what you do, then being a leader becomes much easier.

"Leadership is really about creating an esprit de corps. Creating a sense of a common purpose based on a vision, based on an objective. Coming in here every day could become kind of old after a while unless you create a vision, create a common purpose, create a sense of ownership.

"I love to mentor, and one of the true joys of business is to see people grow. When I interview people, I ask them, 'Do you want my job?' If they answer no, they don't get hired. I want everyone to want my job. One of my former employees, who worked for me for 15 years, told me that when he confronts a challenge in his new company, he says to himself, 'What would Joe do?' And that epitomizes leadership—to empower people, mentor them, and watch them grow."

And good leadership, he says, means not becoming involved in every decision.

"If you're away from the office for three days and have to call eight times, you know you have to change your leadership style. Let go, trust the people around you, and lead as a role model."

When asked about the role of mistakes in running a business, Joe was quite open.

"Ron Rubin told me this many years ago: 'You learn more from your failures than you do from your successes.' That's because business is not a science, it's not formulaic.

"The failures I've encountered in my career revolve more around people than property. You can talk about this business being rooted in bricks and mortar, but the business really rises and falls on people. Early in my career, I probably had more bravado than I should have had. Being young may have been part of that. When you're young, rash, and successful, there's a tendency to wear that on your sleeve and turn people off. That's not the kind of behavior for a leader or team player. My leadership style probably caused some people to either not perform well or to leave the company. I was able to recognize that, become more self-aware, and change my leadership style for the better."

In the future, Coradino sees a focus on smart growth, related to "the greening of America and environmental issues."

"From a real estate perspective, this means that malls will become more vertical, where people can efficiently live, work, shop, dine, and be entertained in the same area, with less impact on the environment. This is also more efficient in serving an aging population."

Beyond his leadership role at PREIT, Coradino is closely involved in giving back to the community.

"I grew up in South Philly. My father used to say, 'Don't go to work with the peppers and eggs under your arm.' He meant don't take your lunch to work, go make money, go be important. Because years ago, when he worked construction, that's how you warmed your lunch on the winter days—you put it under your arm.

"So you go out and make money and become important. But when you've accomplished all that, you end up saying, 'I did it all. What now?' The great example of this is Robert Redford in the movie *The Senator*. He does all that work to become elected, the ticker tape is flying, and he turns to his wife and says, 'What now?' The challenge is to distill meaning from your work and find a larger purpose in it.

"The first generation makes money, and it's hard to give back because you're trying to collect the shekels. But that changes over time, and I started to get a sense of what it's like to give back. I've been on any number of nonprofit boards over the past years, including the Drama Guild, Chestnut Hill College, the YMCAs of Greater Philadelphia, and the Central Philadelphia Development Corporation. There's real happiness and satisfaction that comes from that."

His last words of advice?

"If you own what you do, take responsibility for what you do, and deliver results, then corporate America will acknowledge you."

THE POWER OF ONE

LES COHEN, EXECUTIVE DIRECTOR, KATZ JEWISH COMMUNITY CENTER OF SOUTHERN NEW JERSEY (JCC)

"I subscribe to the power of one theory—that one person can make a difference and move things forward," Les Cohen told me, as we talked in his office. "Imagine the cumulative effect of all of those powers of one coming together? Even though it sounds corny, most of us came into this field because we wanted to build a better world. And I think that we'll build a better world. When we remind ourselves about that, it helps put things in perspective."

Les is CEO of the Katz Jewish Community Center of Southern N.J. (JCC), established in the 1940s in Camden and Pennsauken. As the Center evolved over the years, so did the services offered.

The new JCC, built in 1997, is located in Cherry Hill, N. J., and provides social, cultural, educational, recreational, and health-related programs for the entire community, both secular and non-secular, and serving all age groups. The operating budget is $14 million, with 100 full-time and 700 part-time employees.

"I was a New York City kid who grew up in the projects," Les told me. "The only work I've ever done full time is JCC work.

"I was in college and met someone whose husband worked for JCCs. They were looking for a summer camp supervisor, and I said okay and did it for a couple of summers. Then I got invited to work with teens part time, and eventually that became full time and I started moving up the career ladder."

After earning a master's in counseling psychology and an MSW, Les served in his first executive position with JCC in Norwalk, Connecticut. He worked there for five years, then was offered a consultant position at the national headquarters in New York City. He traveled around the country and Canada, working with JCCs in what he calls "a great learning experience."

When Les joined JCC of Southern N.J. in September, 1990, the organization was testing the waters about building a new facility in a different location. They had already bought a property and begun fundraising, but there were many challenges facing the project.

"The old JCC was literally falling apart. I remember being there a couple of months, and the maintenance chief is out in the lobby looking up at the ceiling and strategically arranging 30-gallon garbage cans.

" 'What are you doing?' I asked him.

" 'It's going to rain tonight,' he said.

"I said, 'Why don't we just fix the roof?' He said they couldn't afford it. So right then I understood the culture. And I said we're going to change this, because nobody wants to be part of a losing organization. Everybody wants to be with a winner and believe in what's happening.

"That was my biggest challenge and maybe my greatest success, because it was very risky for me. I was a young guy. I had three children. I had just moved my family here, and this was the culture I was stepping into. I inherited a $500,000 deficit. If nothing else, we had to be an organization with integrity and that was respected. I didn't want to stay if we couldn't accomplish that.

"The next few years, I worked on things that positioned us in the community, our reputation, and our program. I can remember the first time we did our auction. It was great, first class. I actually heard people say, 'The JCC is doing this?' Because their expectations were so low.

"We held our first Festival of Arts, Books, and Culture and our first auction during the first year I was here. Now it's 20 consecutive years of doing both, with great success. We get 10,000 people coming to our festival, so we've built this reputation and it's wonderful."

Meanwhile, the move to the new location was stalled.

"I was the chief cheerleader for this new building. There were a lot of naysayers who said we'll never raise enough money, or that we'll build it and people won't come, which has happened in some JCC communities. And

I would go into every meeting in the community and say, 'It's going to be wonderful.' You have to believe in the dream."

It took another seven or eight years of fundraising, planning, and dealing with zoning issues, but the new JCC finally opened in 1997.

"We've been here 11 years and it's been a wonderful success story," Les said. "We're a full service Jewish Community Center. We have pre-school and daycare with 300 children. We operate the largest Jewish summer camp in North America, with 1,600 children on a separate site in Medford with 120 acres. We have close to 2,500 older adults taking college level classes taught by university professors. We have an incredible program for children and adults with disabilities, both here and at camp. Two years ago, we expanded our health and wellness department. It's state of the art and has made a tremendous difference in our membership. We've seen our members go up over 1200 units in the last two years."

Les described his leadership style as a combination of "both visionary and hands-on."

"I'm big on building and articulating a consensus vision," he said, "so everyone can get on board about our goals and what JCC is all about. But I'm also very hands on. I'll get down on the floor with the early childhood kids. I'll be out in camp in my shorts, or kibitzing with the senior citizens, or helping to serve them lunch. And that's the beauty of a JCC. I can be both that visionary leader and playing with the kids the next minute. It's really a lot of fun in that respect."

The employee culture at JCC requires shared responsibilities among staff.

"Everyone has more than one job. They have the job they were hired to do, but then they have the bigger job, the crossover job, being part of other activities. We do community-wide events about once a month, and staff are involved even though it may go beyond their specific department. It's really the power of the whole, of all of us coming together. We all get assignments, including me."

To create a motivated and committed organizational culture, Cohen told me that he looks more at the person than at specific skills or a specific job history when hiring.

"Skills are important things, but more important is that they have the hunger to do the job right and the passion to be a part of something bigger than themselves. That's not something we can teach them. We can encourage it, but you've got to be that kind of person to begin with. That's something we've learned the hard way. We'd rather take an enthusiastic person who wants to learn and grow with us, and who's got that hunger to do good, rather than a more experienced person who might be a little bit tired and fixed in doing things a certain way."

For the future, Les is not content with standing still; rather, he wants more of what he calls "crazy ideas"—the innovations and ideas that continue to move an organization forward.

"I'm big on building the team and bringing people together. I will often tell my staff to think creatively, to challenge me with a crazy idea and make it my problem to find the money for it. Because I love those crazy ideas. They become the next big thing for us, the next big 'wow.' We love this 'wow affect'—when people say, 'Wow, look at this place, I can't believe what you're doing.'

"It would be very easy at this point to sit back a little. But I don't think I'd be happy. I want to be able to say, 'What's the next project? What's the next wow that we're doing? And what do we have to do to get there?'"

PUTTING EGOS ASIDE

JOSEPH S. ZURITSKY, CHAIRMAN AND CEO, PARKWAY CORPORATION

During our conversation, Joe Zuritsky described how his parents struggled to make the Parkway Corporation a success.

"My parents started the company with no capital at all," he told me. "They both came from relatively poor families, and they begged and borrowed to get started, but they didn't steal. My parents taught me very good values. I pride myself on maintaining those values and passing them on to the next generation, who are now at work in the company and doing a great job."

Parkway Corporation, still family owned by the second and third generations and headquartered in Philadelphia, is one of only a few U.S. parking companies that operates, designs, and develops parking garages and commercial real estate. The company has about 70 locations with a total of 30,000 parking spaces in five major markets, from Richmond, Va. to Toronto. They own or lease a majority of the facilities they operate. An industry leader in technology integration, Parkway has completely automated the parking process at most of its facilities.

But the company almost went under in the late 1950s and early 1960s, a time when Joe was still in college.

"Because we had no capital back then, my father didn't hesitate to borrow from men who charged unbelievable interest rates," Joe said. "It wasn't the loan sharks that you read about, but they would still charge 30%

to 40% interest. It was really unbelievable. We had a terrible cash flow problem, with more money going out than was coming in.

"One day, we had a momentous meeting with a very big accounting firm to help us straighten things out. We sat with these fellows, all decked out in their suits and ties, and after a couple of hours they concluded there was no hope for the company and counseled us to sell it.

"I had already decided that I wanted to spend my career in this business and wanted to try to build it up, not sell it," Joe went on. "I was in college in those days, and had an accounting professor at Temple University named Marvin Kaufman. We hired him to help us with our problem, and after a very short study he said, 'You have a simple cash flow problem.' In those days, back around 1960, I had never heard the term 'cash flow.' He also said that he had a very simple solution to our problem.

"All we had to do was get long-term debt in the form of mortgages on these properties. He also told us not to worry about the interest rates, because they were deductible. He said we should pay off the short-term loans with the proceeds and thereafter we'd be profitable. He really helped us to understand our errors, and then slowly but surely we started to build the business. During my university and law school days, I worked in the family business every day after school."

Over the last 50 years, Parkway has gone through many evolutions.

"The company has had a number of corporate names over the years," Joe explained. "Early on, it was Fogel's Garage, Inc., which we purchased in the 1950s. It was an old elevator garage and lot located at 235 South 12th Street. At that time, it handled all the cars from the Camac Health Club. The whole Jewish community would go there to play ball, cards, and get massages. We had the parking contract with the health club to handle its patrons.

"We eventually demolished the obsolete garage and built a new office on a part of the land, using the remainder to park additional cars at grade. Slowly but surely we expanded our business, lot by lot, and just as slowly learned how to operate multiple locations by creating an operating organization."

As the company expanded and undertook new risks, it created new corporations to spread the risks, to not jeopardize the older corporations that were beginning to become successful. Some of the corporations created were Minute Wash Corp., Century Garages, Kwik Park Corporation, Parking Facilities, Inc., Parkway Garage, Inc., plus many others. In the 1980s the company changed the name of its primary corporation from Fogel's Garage, Inc. to Parkway Corporation.

As with any business, there were numerous obstacles and setbacks to overcome.

"Believe me, these were hard lessons to learn," Joe said, "because none of us knew anything about running a larger organization. We made many mistakes. Trial and error proved to be the best teacher.

"Then, because I lacked confidence in my own management abilities at that time, I began hiring staff members with good skills but very strong personalities, and ended up with a staff comprised of giant egos. And, of course, they ended up fighting with each other. So half my day was wasted keeping peace and the other half was spent on business.

"From this I learned that it's difficult to run a business with people who have big egos. We needed people with good skills, but who are also team players. People who enjoyed working with other staff and working for the success of the venture."

At the same time, Joe said the company was taking "some giant chances."

"When you're small and you don't have a lot to lose, you're tempted to take bigger chances. If you guess right, you survive, and if you guess wrong, you go under. In the early 1970s we had grown quite a bit, but didn't yet have a good functioning organization, so I ended up doing virtually everything.

"For about eight years, I was working seven days and seven nights," Joe told me. "I checked the lots day and night. Hired every employee, fired them, chased after new locations, watched the numbers, and literally ran myself ragged. We'd been going to the National Parking Convention every year since I was a young teenager and we'd bring back new ideas. Both dad and I loved innovation, and slowly but surely we implemented these new approaches and upgraded our business. As time went on, other Philadelphia parking operators began to watch and imitate us. As a result, the entire Philadelphia industry operates smarter today because of our methods.

"Because of my work 'overload,' I decided to bring in a national company and let them take over our leased and managed locations, and we kept all but a couple of locations for ourselves. It was an intermediate step where I could catch my breath and figure out what we should do next."

At that time, Joe said the company made a major deal that helped transform its entire existence. They outbid two major companies by about $50,000 on a $4.5 million bid to acquire the leasehold interest for the Love Park underground garage. Because of the garage's parking rate structure, Parkway realized that the garage was not being managed correctly. It was filling up at 9 a.m. and turning cars away the rest of the day.

"Dad and I sat down and struggled with this. Out of the 800 spaces, 500 cars were parking all day. We realized we must do something radical. We got the Parking Authority to agree to let us raise the daily rate from $2.50 to $3.30. It was the largest one-time raise in the history of Philadelphia. In those days, you'd raise rates a nickel or a dime at a time, and a quarter raise was considered outrageous. As we planned, this radical increase chased half of the all-day cars out of the garage, so 250 of those 500 all-day cars were gone.

"Now we had room for the daytime traffic. We took those 250 spaces and parked in them a total of 750 cars daily. Suddenly, for the first time in its history, the garage realized a profit, and from that point on we just kept moving that garage upward. A year later we built our first self-park garage at 16th and Ludlow to Ranstead Streets, one of the first in Philadelphia in those days." This garage was later sold to Bill Rouse, and it then became the rear portion of the current CIGNA building site.

Zuritsky told me that Parkway is implementing new and improved technology all the time and considers itself way ahead of the rest of the industry. He cited his involvement with a 31-story condo building that has a robotic garage in the basement, where cars are parked automatically in an underground storage system on computer-operated pallets.

In his leadership style, Joe delegates and doesn't micromanage.

"I'm not a controlling person," he said. "I don't have that in my personality. I need to have faith in my employees. That's really what counts. When I think we should go left instead of right, I voice it, but I listen to our people and respect them, because that's why they're here. It doesn't mean, though, that they get to make every decision or that every opinion they have is right or is followed by me.

"What I really enjoy is creating. Every time we buy a property, we put our stamp on it, whether it remains in parking or is further developed. That's very satisfying, especially when things work out the way we've planned. As a company, we don't try to get an edge on our partners. We enjoy our success, but we can also enjoy theirs. It's very much a 'live and let live' attitude."

Joe's son, Robert, is now president of the company and runs the day-to-day business, although Joe remains very involved in every aspect of operations, especially real estate development. He spends some of his time in civic and charitable matters, as the company currently supports over 100 organizations.

"I really enjoy trying to do good. That's something else that I inherited from my parents. I'm involved with many, many charitable organizations.

Currently, I'm excited by the new National Museum of American Jewish History, which is being built at Fifth and Market.

"I am very pleased with where we are today," Joe concluded. "Luck has always played a role. As good as you think you and your team are, you need good luck. I really believe that. And so far, we've had good fortune."

PROVIDING A SERVICE WE TAKE FOR GRANTED

DON CORRELL,
PRESIDENT AND CEO,
AMERICAN WATER

For much of this country's history, the state and Federal governments did not provide water service to communities. Instead, private companies were granted franchises to become water utilities, and back in the early 19th century nine out of ten water systems were built by private enterprise. It was only during the late 1800s that municipal entities began to buy their water systems to manage growth. Today, 85% of Americans get their water from a municipality, not from a company like American Water.

"Like everyone else, I took water for granted as much as anyone else when I was young," said Don Correll, the company's President and CEO, during our meeting at the company's headquarters in Voorhees, N.J. "We're to water what a utility would be to electricity. We serve 15 million people in 32 states and Canada."

Founded in 1886, America Water is the largest investor-owned (NYSE: AWK) water and wastewater utility company in the U.S., with revenues of more than $2.3 billion in 2008 and 7000 employees. Most of its business in the last 50 years has been concentrated in suburban areas, like Cherry Hill, N.J., and the suburbs of Pittsburgh and St. Louis.

Correll grew up in Lehigh Valley, a Phillies fan hoping to make the major leagues, "but neither my height nor my hitting prowess was going to get me there."

Don studied accounting and finance as an undergraduate, and then earned an MBA in finance. He started out in public accounting, worked for a water utility in the finance area, and after 15 years became its president. He served there for 10 years, growing it into the second largest water utility after American Water. He became CEO of American Water in April, 2006.

I asked Don about his path to becoming CEO. Was it a straight line? Had he always aspired to the position?

"I think everybody has to have a five-year plan: where do you want to be in five years? When you're 26 or 27, your plan isn't necessarily to become a CEO, especially when the people running your company are in their 40s or 50s. But I set some goals for myself. I knew I needed more management experience and more education. I went back to school at night and got an MBA in finance. Then I made another five-year plan and worked toward it."

Correll looked for opportunities to take on more responsibility.

"My company recognized that I wanted to take on more, and they were willing to work with me and challenge me. I had mentors and I worked with evolving challenges, whether it was building a new water supply, dealing with rate increases or droughts, or positioning the company for growth."

Correll emphasized how his career was helped by good mentors, "people who served as sounding boards, and who understood that business is not just about capital, but managing people and giving them opportunities. That was critical."

Correll recalled one mentor who was a big influence when he was in his late 20s and just starting out in the business.

"This man was in his 60s, an interim CEO, a very calm, focused, and accomplished person. He had already left his mark on one organization, and was there to see this company through a five or seven-year period. He was a mentor to the entire team. He saw me as someone who could accomplish more, if I had the opportunity and the oversight and the trust. And I learned from him how to build a team and give people opportunity within an organization. You can't do everything yourself. It's not going to happen. You have to have the right people working for you. You have to trust them and they have to know that you trust them. And you have to hold them accountable—they have to know they're in their positions to get something done. I learned all this from that mentor, and I've worked in the same way for 30 years."

Crucial to his daily work as CEO is staying in touch with his senior management team.

"I touch base with the top ten people in the organization at least once every other day, if not every day. I prefer face-to-face, next would be telephone. Last for me is sending an email. I haven't reached the point where I find it personal enough. It's just as easy to pick up the phone. I hear their voices and they hear mine. It's the next closest thing to meeting them face-to-face. I'm also an absolute subscriber to management by walking around (MBWA). When you have face time, you know you're connecting with someone. I fear the day when the majority of communication is through the internet, because then we've lost the personal touch."

Correll's vision of the company's future sees an increased role for the private sector in supplying water.

"The idea for the last century that one answer fits all—that the local entity or town owns it and runs it—isn't the only answer. We've had a lot of successes in the last few years demonstrating that we can work with those public entities that have owned their water systems for 20 or 100 years. They have to build a new plant, but they realize they don't have to do it the way they've always done it. Or they realize they don't have to provide water service, when they also need to do fire, safety, and education.

"With the country $11 trillion in debt, with another trillion a year as far as the eye can see, and with $2.5 trillion in municipal debt across the country, from basically zero in 1950, there's going to be an inflection point. I don't know if that's going to happen next year or over the next decade, but that's where I see our company using its strength and its history to work with government entities and municipalities to show that there is another way."

Complementing this financial and political rationale, American Water has the resources and technology to make water systems more efficient, particularly for those small communities that lack large resources or infrastructure to deal with water issues.

"We bring technology to every aspect of our business, whether treating water, reading meters, or detecting leaks in the system. We work with R&D groups that have new technology that might help with a specific problem in West Virginia because of the terrain there, or with a water quality problem in New Mexico. A small municipal entity of 25,000 people in Pennsylvania or Ohio or Kentucky doesn't have the same ability to focus on these types of problems. There aren't a lot of mayors who stay up at night because of a water issue. They're thinking about teacher contracts, budget issues, or the next election."

I asked Don how he handled the inevitable stress that comes with being a CEO.

"If I show stress, then everybody else in the organization will. I have good genes from my father, who was a very relaxed and calm individual. I've seen a lot and learned a lot. But there are certain things you can't control, and there's no point in getting stressed about them. I find the job enormously rewarding and enjoy the interaction with all the people I work with."

Correll doesn't dispute that there have been corporate excesses in recent years.

"Has it gone over the top? I absolutely agree with that. I wouldn't want to take anything away from entrepreneurship and rewards for performance, but there were some outsized executive bonuses in years past that boggle the mind."

Summing up, Correll emphasized the service his company supplies, one often taken for granted by the public.

"The bottled water industry did an effective job of selling the convenience, while creating a taint about tap water. As an industry, we were outraged 20 years ago when they started doing it. Some bottled water is more expensive than a gallon of gas, but the cost to the company is less than a penny. A terrific markup, if you can do it, but that's not our business. We're not marketers—we're service providers. We take the water, clean it, and deliver it to your house."

I glanced at the bottle of water that Don had offered me when I first walked in, which the company gives out at community events (American Water doesn't sell water retail).

"Don't worry," Correll reassured me, laughing. "That's our water. We'd forbid anything else."

KEEPING IT IN PERSPECTIVE

JOSEPH FRICK, PRESIDENT AND CEO, INDEPENDENCE BLUE CROSS

"We've always been a mission driven organization," Joe Frick told me. "From our creation 71 years ago, we were the insurer of last resort for many people. We're not a national company, so we've always had community roots. We're not a publicly traded stock company, so it was never about making big margins. It was always about touching as many people as possible and making a small margin that could be reinvested in the community."

Independence Blue Cross and its subsidiaries are the Philadelphia region's largest health insurers, with more than 2.6 million members locally and 3.3 million overall. The company employs nearly 5,500 people, annually processes more than 26 million claims, and responds to more than 5 million customer inquiries. Joe, who joined the company in 1993, has been CEO since January 2005.

As part of its commitment to the community, Independence Blue Cross conducts a variety of programs and activities to help address the health needs of the uninsured. In 2009, IBC supported 36 private, non-profit health clinics that annually provide free care to more than 110,000 uninsured adults and children in Southeastern Pennsylvania, and invested more than $40 million to help hold down the cost of providing health insurance to low-income adults and children.

"I'm having a tough time with the healthcare reform debate," Joe told me. "I know the current model is not sustainable and I'm as pro-reform as it gets, but when it went from healthcare reform to health insurance reform, all of us in the business, even if we're non-profit, got painted with a broad brush. We're seen as doing bad things to raise profits, when that's not the case. That's been tough on our employees.

"Being people-centered is at my core," Joe went on. "Maybe to a fault. It's probably tougher for me, given my background in human resources positions, to make tough decisions regarding people, because I spent my whole career investing in them."

One of his most difficult days occurred when a large number of employees took voluntary early retirement in the fall of 2009.

"We were saying goodbye to 531 people, representing 11,350 years of service to our company. Gut wrenching. Especially because I knew all these people, and had worked with them. So that morning, people were crying. They were pleased that our company had a progressive way to right size. They felt good about their decision, but it was tough to leave."

When I asked Frick if he was a natural leader as a kid, he cited the importance of education as a formative experience in his life.

"My mom and dad were both from Philly. They were not college-educated, but they did everything they could to make sure that their three boys got a top-flight education. We all attended Catholic schools in Baltimore, even though my mom had to go to work to enable us to do that. I was the first in my family to go to college."

Frick then attended Notre Dame, which he considers "a very special place."

"It was incredibly values-laden," he said. "It was a tremendous environment to learn and grow. I developed an extraordinary sense of purpose and mission.

"But when you say natural leader, I've never viewed myself as that. Rather, I've viewed myself as kind of a galvanizing force, an energizing influence. I've always had the ability to get groups of folks enthusiastic about things. People have always gravitated to me as an organizer or facilitator. So I've never taken myself seriously and it's never been about me. It's always been about the cause or the institution or the organization."

When Frick once took a career aptitude test, he was "off the charts" to be a funeral director.

"When I talked to a group at Wharton last week, I said how about that? Funeral director? But I told them that when I look back on it now, it makes sense. I have the ability to help people feel a sense of calm, stability, and reassurance during times of anxiety and turbulence. That's important for a leader."

After executive positions with Westinghouse and the *Philadelphia Inquirer* and *Daily News*, Frick joined Independence Blue Cross at a time of major expansion for the company.

"That first year was a whirlwind. My role was to help Fred DiBona move this organization forward, to perhaps develop a different operating model, while retaining the same philosophy and values, and that's what we did. For the first five years we were experiencing phenomenal growth. In the mid-1990s we almost doubled our size and scope."

A large part of Joe's story involves his personal health crisis. At age 55 in 2007, he was diagnosed with stage three colon cancer.

"It was like, 'Oh my God, what are you saying to me, Lord?' But you know what? It ended up being a kind of gift. It was just another challenge to deal with, but one that gave me an incredible perspective. It enabled me to see my company and the healthcare system through the eyes of the patient.

"When you're faced with your own mortality, it changes everything," Joe went on. "I went down to pick up my daughter after her first year of college, expecting to give her a hug and say I'm proud of you, and instead I had to say, 'Kate, I have cancer and it's pretty serious.'

"I remember those two hours. Then she and I had to get in the car and drive to my parents to tell them. She sobbed the whole way back to Philadelphia. So many things were going through my mind. Am I going to see her get married? Am I going to see my kids graduate?"

Frick underwent surgery and very aggressive chemotherapy.

"My chemo was pretty debilitating. I lost 55 pounds in 90 days. I had 24 weeks of hell, but the health care staff who supported me were terrific. So far I've been healthy for 2½ years. So far, so good.

"I'm healthier from a physical, emotional, and spiritual standpoint. I'm a pretty emotional guy, so it's helped me to stay a little more even keeled. I still have a port in my chest, so when I'm having a bad meeting or bad day, I put my hand on my port. It gives me perspective and keeps me where I need to be."

Joe has since joined an organization called the CEO Roundtable on Cancer.

"It's made up of CEOs from all around the country, many who have been touched by cancer in some way, and who are doing everything they can within their organizations to prevent cancer and support people who are dealing with it."

In closing, Joe said the following:

"I'm more and more convinced that we have a responsibility, as leaders, to have a personal brand that's impeccable because people want to feel good about their companies and their leaders, particularly when you read about inappropriate business or personal conduct that taints our whole profession.

"The day we all take ourselves too seriously is the day that we shouldn't be leading anymore. Our job is to create an environment where people can achieve their personal and professional potential, by being part of a mission-driven organization."

THE PERSONAL TOUCH

ROBERT SOPER, PRESIDENT AND CEO, MOHEGAN SUN AT POCONO DOWNS

(Winner of the 2009 CEO of the Year Award for the Human Resources Department of the Year Awards, which I created)

When Bobby Soper earned his law degree from the University of Georgia, he already had a job lined up in Atlanta. But he had family with the Mohegan Sun organization in southeast Connecticut, operated by the Mohegan Tribe, and a cousin asked him to consider joining the company.

"So I went up to Connecticut," Bobby told me. "The casino had just opened, and I was wowed by the whole thing." In 1997, Soper joined Mohegan Sun as in-house legal counsel.

"I really enjoyed it. I was able to work with some of the best law firms in the country and do things that most attorneys fresh out of law school could never do. For example, I was able to take part in raising billions of dollars in financing and developing new projects."

Over time Soper worked with Mohegan Sun's CEO, got to know the operations, and ultimately became a senior vice president. In 2005, when Mohegan purchased Pocono Downs in Plains, Pa., which ultimately became the state's first casino, Soper became its CEO.

While Soper didn't imagine himself becoming a chief executive as a child, he was ambitious and always involved in politics and school organizations.

"In high school, I was president of two or three organizations. I had a leadership kind of style, but I always thought it was going to take me into politics. My aspirations were to become a U.S. Senator or a similar career, and I actually spent some time in D.C. one summer during college, but I learned from that experience that a political career wasn't really for me.

"College teaches you a lot of things about what your interests are, and I found that economics was my passion. An ideal job for me after I retire would be to teach economics."

When I asked Bobby what influenced his philosophy of leadership, he mentioned a mentor.

"The individual who not only gave me these opportunities, but who also molded me, was my boss, Bill Velardo, who unfortunately passed away just two months ago. He really taught me the most important attributes of leadership. Not only taught me, but he showed me through example.

"Leadership is about respect. It's about humility. It's about objectivity and not being emotional. For me, those attributes differentiate the great leaders from the ones who are merely good. Many leaders have great experience and background, but ego often gets in their way."

I asked Soper if a more intimidating or aggressive style might sometimes be necessary in certain business situations.

"In the long run, that style never works. This doesn't mean you shouldn't make decisions or be direct. But you also need to listen and communicate with respect. It's more challenging to master, because it takes time and patience. I'm fortunate I have my mom's genes, so patience is a little easier to practice. It's in my genetic make-up, though it still can be a great challenge at times.

"I take the team approach. If there's trash on the floor, I'm as responsible as the attendant. If there's a security concern, I'm as responsible as the security officer. And most importantly, we're all responsible for providing service and accommodating our guests. Everyone's door is open. No one has their own turf, so I expect everybody to share information. I trust the decisions of my team and they know that."

I asked Soper what method he uses to hire the right person for that type of culture. Is it gut instinct? A particular kind of process?

"I think the philosophy is the same, whether you're hiring the vice president or an attendant who cleans the floor. We believe in a personality-based approach. Simply put, you can't fake good service. Either you enjoy making people happy and serving them, or you don't. Part of the hiring process is trying to decipher who truly enjoys serving others and who doesn't.

"No matter how smart they are, how experienced, or even how successful they've been, if I don't think they have the right personality to make a good fit, I'm not going to hire them. I'm not always right, and when that happens it's my responsibility to make sure they depart. There is no compromise there."

I asked Soper if there were other secrets that make an organization successful.

"When you have a great culture and your team members have high morale, it will translate into good customer service, which then translates into customer loyalty and bottom line profit. That's why we focus so much on developing and sustaining a culture of mutual respect, teamwork, and having fun. One thing I tell every new team member is this: when you wake up and you don't want to come in, don't come in. It's not fair to you and it's not fair to the organization."

I pointed out to Soper how one wrong hire can create a toxic environment in an organization, if given the opportunity.

"It is absolutely amazing how negativity can spread so much quicker than something positive," he agreed. "Part of maintaining a positive culture is making sure that upper level management is in the trenches. You've got to be in the trenches to have a true sense of what's going on. You can hear about your operations all you want from your supervisors, but unless you see it and feel it, interact with customers when things are bad or when things are busy, you can lose touch with your organization. This principle applies at all times. I'm here on Christmas Day, I'm here on New Year's Day, and I'm here on Thanksgiving Day. I may not spend all day, but I'm going to try to interact with team members from every shift so I can thank them for coming in.

"The point is to be visible and always responsive. You don't always have the right answer, and you don't always have the answer they want to hear, but you always respond."

Soper believes in communicating that message through a personal connection.

"Any time you have an opportunity to make an emotional deposit, you should take advantage of that opportunity. It may be on the floor, it may be on the phone, or it may be through email. There will be times when you have no choice but to make an emotional withdrawal. You do it as nicely as you can, but inevitably you have to make withdrawals. So, any time you have a chance to make a deposit, you do it. Pat somebody on the back and tell them they did a good job.

"That doesn't mean you don't make tough decisions in order to sustain your business. In the long term, though, every decision you make has to help sustain your culture."

Soper pointed out that communication with employees is especially crucial in the casino business, where high revenues can lead to misunderstandings.

"Our great challenge in the casino environment is that we deal with big numbers. We generate $250 million in revenue in this one property, but it's a very low margin business, especially in a high tax environment like Pennsylvania. It's also a very capital intensive business—the investment is over a half billion dollars and the return on investment is spread out over a long period of time.

"But employees can fail to understand the financial structure and financial model. If you do $250 million, why is there a salary freeze or a 401K pullback? When you make those decisions during a tough period, you have to be very careful on how you communicate. And it's challenging to communicate to the mass of team members effectively, whether it's a beverage server or a cashier or a security officer. How do you communicate the big picture? That's always the challenge in this business."

Soper explained his view of success from the CEO perspective.

"For me, there's no greater measurement of success than having someone from my team grow and be promoted. For example, a vice president on my team moved on to capitalize on a great opportunity paying three times what he gets now and with much greater responsibility. Although it's painful for him to leave, it's also a great success. If someone's going to leave, that's how I want it to happen. His success is a little bit of a reflection on me, too. The same applies when someone or something doesn't work out—that's a failure on my part."

Soper returned to the personal touch when I asked him for his advice to aspiring leaders.

"What differentiates great leaders from good leaders is remarkably simple. It's the simple stuff of building relationships and taking the time, all those little things day in and day out. When someone comes in your office, take your eyes off the computer and look at him and talk to him. It's about telling people you care. It's the soft skills. You don't earn respect by generating a 22% margin this year versus a 20% margin last year. You're going to have good years and bad years. In the long run, your respect is earned by how you treated your team members, your guests, your vendors, and everyone else throughout your career.

"One of the things I do, and I admit it can sometimes be time consuming and challenging, is to respond personally to letters sent to my attention. We receive many letters all the time, good and bad, and I respond to every single one. Some weeks, I'll handwrite 25 or 30 responses. Over time, that makes a huge difference. I'll have guests say to me, 'You know what? I wrote you a letter and you wrote me back. I really appreciated that.' I hear it from people all the time."

A QUESTION OF BALANCE

MARY STENGEL AUSTEN, PRESIDENT AND CEO, TIERNEY GROUP

At age 24 in 1989, Mary Stengel Austen co-founded the Tierney Group with Brian Tierney and a third person. Today, the Tierney Group is one of the mid-Atlantic region's largest full-service communications firms, providing both advertising and PR services to a range of industry leaders, including Bayer Environmental Science, Fox Chase Cancer Center, Independence Blue Cross, McDonald's, PECO, the Pennsylvania Tourism Office, Sun Life Financial, TD Bank, and Verizon Wireless. The firm has 140 employees based in Philadelphia, with a satellite office in Harrisburg.

Mary told me she was drawn to leadership roles from a young age.

"I played field hockey and lacrosse. I was the captain of the cheerleaders, which some people really torture me about. I was the president of my sorority at Lafayette College in Easton, Pennsylvania."

Austen double majored in English and government and law. She loved to write and began to look for positions where she could use that talent.

"I was looking for an internship in advertising at a company in Philadelphia called Spiro & Associates," Mary told me. "They said they didn't have any advertising internships. My father worked in sales and marketing, and, ironically, the agency that he used was Spiro, and a man at the firm, Gordon Lawrence, was my father's account management person.

But I was a kid who was going to do this on my own and I didn't want to use my father's name.

"So I didn't use the connection, and I got the internship. I was there for two or three weeks, I get in the elevator, and there's Mr. Lawrence. I didn't know him well, so I introduced myself and told him I was an intern in PR. He said, 'You didn't call me?'

"He was really hurt, I think. Today, I would counsel my kids that it's crazy not to use a connection. If people I know call and ask me to meet with their son or daughter, I do it. It doesn't necessarily mean they're going to get the job or the internship.

"Gordon Lawrence worked on the advertising side, I was on the PR side," Mary continued. "He encouraged me to meet with him to learn more about his accounts and that side of the business. He said if you really like to write, you'll get a chance to do that. I was writing bylined articles and I loved the diversity of the work. I was an intern over the summer. In September they hired me as a freelance writer, and in October I was brought on full time as an associate account executive."

Mary also had a mentorship relationship with Brian Tierney.

"He was 31 and I was 24 years old when we co-founded the company. Both of us were semi-kids but he was definitely a mentor.

"Early on, we had a big pitch for Marriott. I might have been with the firm for two weeks. We were on our way to make the presentation, and Brian was asking me for my opinion. He really meant it. He wasn't saying, 'Oh, let me just ask her because I think she'll like me to ask her.' He really wanted me to tell him what I thought. He was very interested in hearing from people who were not necessarily in senior positions. It didn't really matter whether you were 22 or 32 or 42. Were you smart, could you think on your feet, were you curious? Brian always wanted me to learn more, dig deeper.

"That attitude has stuck with me, and hopefully that's how I treat other people."

Jack Welch is another person who taught Mary about the value of mentors.

"I met him four or five years ago and he was what I expected—kind of gruff, aggressive, but very direct. The first thing he said to me was, 'Tell me about your business' and the second question was, 'Who are your mentors?' When I told him, he said, 'You have only two people as mentors?' I said, 'Well, people are busy,' and he said, 'That's stupid.' I was walking back to the elevator and I said to a colleague, 'I think Jack Welch just called me stupid.'

But he was right. Welch said, 'First of all, if you ask somebody to be your mentor and they say no, you don't want that person to be your mentor because they're not good people. If you don't ask, you don't get. If you want to grow, if you want to learn more about your field, you have to take a chance.'

"So I started reaching out to people to mentor me. Quite frankly, it also helps on the client prospecting side, too."

I asked Mary if it was harder to lead as a woman. Was it the same playing field?

"I would say it is the same probably 90% of the time. Men and women are built differently in terms of their makeup, but I think we have many of the same desires, issues, distractions, and frustrations. I don't feel I've ever been taken less seriously because I'm a woman. In other disciplines, maybe. There are so many women in communications. If I were in manufacturing, it might be a different story.

"No matter who you are, you have to prove yourself to clients. You have to be able to go toe-to-toe. You have to be able to put in the same amount of work. And then you have to manage the family piece. People will say to me, 'How do you have five kids and run a business?'"

With four boys and a girl, ages 6 to 13, Mary is very sensitive to how family issues affect employees.

"I've taken maternity leave, and I've also managed people who are having babies," she said. "We do have flexible work situations, but you also can't take advantage of it. Even when I was out on maternity leave, if I had a major meeting, I had to be here.

"Has flexibility helped in the work place? Absolutely. But many women don't have the resources that I do. When I had my first child, my mother took care of my son for the first year and a half. Not all women have the same option. If you don't have a support network or sufficient economic means, you can't make that choice. Either you have to go to work or you have to stay home."

Mary had been able to find balance between her career and raising her family.

"Some people ask, 'Why are you doing this? Do you feel that you're missing something? Do you have any regrets?'

"I really don't have any regrets. I'm not going to say it isn't challenging to figure out what takes priority. How do you achieve balance? Some days it's business, some days it's personal. You have to just make decisions.

"If your child's in the hospital, that's obviously going to be your priority. But if you have a major business presentation and you can't get to the baseball game, that's an opportunity to have a dialogue with your kid and say, 'You know what? I've been to the other three and I'd love to be at this one, but I can't.'"

For the future, Austen is focused on bringing along a new generation of leaders, people who can "take our place and challenge us."

"You get better and better at tennis if you're playing other people who are better," she said. "It's sometimes easy to get comfortable, and that to me is a danger sign. It doesn't have to be counterproductive to have people who will challenge and question and push."

ALWAYS MORE THAN A TRANSACTION

BILL MCDERMOTT,
CO-CEO,
MEMBER EXECUTIVE
BOARD, SAP AG

Bill McDermott was appointed Co-CEO of SAP on February 7, 2010. In this capacity, and also as a member of the Executive Board of SAP, he oversees the German software developer's strategic business activities relative to all customer operations, sales, marketing, communications, field services (consulting), corporate development, and ecosystem activities.

McDermott was first named to the SAP Executive Board in 2008 to manage global field operations, a responsibility he continues to maintain as Co-CEO. During this time, McDermott has been instrumental in re-architecting the company's go-to-market strategy, closely aligning the field organizations and product development teams, led by co-CEO Jim Hagemann Snabe.

Prior to this role on the SAP Executive Board, he led SAP's operations in the Americas (United States, Canada, and Latin America) and Asia Pacific Japan regions. Since his arrival in 2002, the company has delivered unparalleled growth in market share, revenue, and customer satisfaction in key markets.

Previously Bill served as executive vice president at Siebel Systems, president of Gartner, Inc., and enjoyed a 17-year-career with Xerox. McDermott has received numerous awards for his achievements and leadership in the business world, and for his contributions to community affairs.

The story of Bill's rise to the top of the corporate world exemplifies, as well as summarizes, the core values of entrepreneurship described in this book—a positive attitude, a relentless work ethic, and always putting the customer first.

Born in Flushing, New York, and the oldest of four kids, Bill grew up in Amityville, Long Island. His dad worked for Con Edison and his mom was mostly a homemaker.

"I was a hard worker as a kid," Bill recalled. "My first job was delivering papers. I can remember my mom vouching for me. 'Even though he's really young,' she'd say, 'he's really committed and will deliver the goods.'

"I was 15 when I applied for my first serious job at Finest Supermarkets in Amityville. I think it was $3.65 an hour back then.

"I waited on line and when I got to the front, they said thank you very much, you're kind of young, most people who get these jobs will be adults. I spotted this guy in a green coat who looked important, so I went over to him and said, 'I'm Bill McDermott. I really want to work. I might be the youngest one, but I'll hustle. I'll give you a full day.'

"No sooner did I arrive home then I got a phone call from the man: 'Be here tomorrow after school.' Then I got my second job as a busboy at Amato's, an Italian restaurant in Amityville. I had discretionary time, particularly on the weekends, so I took a third job with the Town of Amityville, picking up garbage, painting fences, doing things like that. So now I had three jobs going for me.

"Nobody was pushing me, nobody was nudging me. This is what I wanted to do. It wasn't work to me. It was fun and I loved getting ahead. I got my own car and clothes, and contributed around the house.

"So one day I'm leaving the restaurant and I see a sign in a delicatessen window, help wanted. I walk in wearing my tuxedo from Amato's restaurant, looking like I'm part of a wedding celebration. I asked the owner what kind of help he was looking for. He said, 'Well, I need somebody who gives good customer service, handles food well, and brings some professionalism to the store.' I said, 'You've met your man. When can I start?' And I started the next day.

"Soon I was working 90 to 100 hours a week in the deli and I had to drop the other three jobs. I was the owner's number two guy.

"Eventually the owner and his partner decided to sell the deli to a TV repairman who realizes he doesn't want to run it. I go on vacation with my family and the store gets robbed. The new owner decides to sell the business to me. And I'm still in high school.

"I bought the business for notes, no cash, with the understanding that if I don't pay off the notes in a year, the previous owner gets the business back. If I pay off the notes in a year or sooner, I'm all set, it's my business.

"Since I didn't have a lot of money, I got the meat man, the beer man, and all the suppliers to put their first orders on the shelves on consignment. I said, 'I know you'll charge me a little too much, but we're in business right?' They took a chance because they knew what I could do.

"Then I saw a market for video games, Pacman, Asteroids, and all that. They were $4,000 apiece then, so I couldn't to buy them. I convinced the guy who owns the machines to give me three of them. I said, 'We'll split the quarters, you get half and I get half.' My brother built a game room, we put the machines in there, and we paid off the loans in no time. I was able to go to high school at the same time because my family and friends were able to work shifts and help me out. We built that deli into a nice business, and I learned a lot of valuable lessons that have served me well to this day.

"Number one, it's all about the customer. You have to focus on your customer and deliver better service than anyone else. People like to say that, but a lot of time there's not much substance behind it. They think they're supposed to say that because they went to management school and somebody told them to say it. But I know it because I had to live it.

"When you have a little business and you don't have too much money and you're going up against 7-Eleven a block away, you say to yourself, 'How am I going to survive? These guys have more money, more resources, a better business model, all the things that I don't have.'

"Two, you have to segment your market very effectively. I had basically three market segments. One was the high school kid. I had to get him to walk past the 7-Eleven a block away and come to my store. What was my hook? Video games. In addition, 7-Eleven only let kids in the store four at a time. It's very annoying when you treat kids like thieves. If you treat them like they're not going to be honest, they're either going to steal stuff anyway or they're going to walk down to my store. I let them in 40 at a time. No problem.

"Blue collar workers were my second market, because they're good with a buck. You see, they get paid on Friday and are broke by Sunday, so I gave them credit. I had their names written in a notebook, and I let them take whatever they wanted—sandwiches, cigarettes, beer—during the week. When they got paid on Friday, they paid me in cash that night. I never got beat out of a single dollar. When you treat people with dignity and respect, you get it back.

"The third market was senior citizens. They don't like to leave the house, so we delivered while 7-Eleven didn't.

"None of this was a massive stroke of genius," Bill said. "It was simply realizing that I couldn't make payroll, pay the rent, and pay off the note unless I took care of my customers better than anybody else."

McDermott also realized another important lesson—that the little things you do in business mean a lot and go a long way.

"What I learned from being a busboy at Amato's was to dress beautifully in the deli. When you cut people's meat, wear white gloves with plastic over them so people see you're handling their food with respect. The floors had to be clean enough to eat off. We waxed them every night. You don't let a woman walk to the car with groceries, with her kids following behind. You carry the groceries for her and help them into the car. When you show respect, it permeates the entire organization."

I asked Bill how he made the transition from small business owner to major positions in the corporate world.

"Thanks to my mom and dad, I went to Dowling College in Oakdale, Long Island, full-time while I was still doing the deli. I did homework when I had lull time behind the slicer. I sold the deli when I graduated from college and got my parents a beach house in Myrtle Beach, South Carolina. A successful exit strategy. You don't make millions, but you're okay.

"Then I went to work for Xerox and that's how my ambition evolved. I never intended to slice bologna for the rest of my life. That was a means to an end. I wanted to be a corporate leader. At the time, Xerox had one of the best training programs in the world.

"I got an interview with Xerox in Manhattan. I get through all the screens and have several interviews. I'm sitting in the waiting room in a $99 suit from the mall and I see these other kids in their Brooks Brothers suits. You could see the Ivy League polish, and I realized that this was a different world. I thought to myself, 'I have one thing they don't have. I want it so much more than they do.'

"So after four very good interviews I'm on the waiting list and get to see the top guy, Emerson Forward. He was the top manager in New York for Xerox at that time. I walk into his office after I cleared the secretarial screen. I'd been waiting at least an hour by this point.

"We sit down and have a great conversation, and at the end Forward says, 'I never heard of Dowling College.'

"I told him about the school. And then he says, 'Bill, look, this has been a great week. I really mean it. The HR department is going to be in touch and I wish you a lot of luck.'

"I said, 'Mr. Forward, in all due respect, I don't think you completely understand or that I've completely communicated the promise that I made this morning.'

"'What do you mean?'

"'Well,' I said, 'my dad drove me to the railroad tracks in Amityville, Long Island, this morning, and I made a promise that I was coming home tonight with my employee badge in my pocket. I've never broken a promise to my father in 22 years and I can't start now.' I was as serious then as I am now.

"Forward broke out laughing. 'Bill McDermott,' he said, 'as long as you haven't committed any crimes, you're hired. That was an unbelievable close.'

"'No,' I said, 'I just told you the truth.' Because that's exactly what I told my father that morning when he took me to the train tracks. And I imagined a positive outcome that morning. I never went into any situation where I did not imagine a positive outcome beforehand.

"I started at Xerox that summer. I was 22. I started out knocking on cold doors in New York City. I was selling copiers, electronic typewriters, fax machines. I had to really know my doormen. I had to know my buildings. I had to know who the screens were and how to get past them. You had to have a relentless work ethic, because New York is a tough place if you're looking for people to pat you on the fanny and tell you everything's going to be okay. So you thicken up pretty quick, but I just loved it. I think that I learned a lot from Xerox, and Xerox maybe learned a thing or two from me. It was a good match."

We talked a little about the art of salesmanship.

"I'll give you an example of the difference between being a book smart sales person who went through spin training," Bill said, "and an authentic salesman who's comfortable in his own skin.

"When I was a trainee, I went on a sales call with a guy named Bob Ryan. I got to carry his bag and see how he did it. So we go into a brownstone in Manhattan. It's August, it's real hot, and the elevator isn't working, so we had to walk up four or five flights of stairs. A woman ran her own business at the brownstone, so Bob's going in there to do the sales thing.

"Across the room is this huge cat. I'm wearing my navy blue suit, financed on credit, of course. The cat loves to jump on people and lands on my left shoulder. It's grabbing onto my suit with its claws and I'm like, 'Oh man, there goes that suit I just financed.'

"So the lady looks at me and goes, 'Do you like cats?'"

"'I really do like cats,' I told her, 'and I don't think Garfield has anything on this one.'

"'Oh, you like cats? Tell me about your pets.'

"And we get into a pet conversation. Very authentic, just an enjoyable conversation.

"Meanwhile, Bob's getting frustrated because we've spent 35 minutes talking about cats. The product hasn't come out of the bag yet. So Bob says, 'Bill, I think it's time now that we do the demonstration on the copier and typewriter.'

"I looked at the woman and said, 'Do you need one?'

"And she says, 'I'll take both of them. Where do I sign?' She signs, we walk out.

"We hit the sidewalk and I said, 'Bob, here's the slip.'

"'McDermott,' he said, 'you're either going to be the CEO of Xerox or you're going to jail.'

"I said, 'Bob, that was just two people having an authentic conversation.'"

McDermott worked his way up in Xerox from a door-to-door salesman to an account executive. At 24, he got his first sales team and covered a large part of Manhattan.

He eventually ran the New York region as the sales operations manager, went to Puerto Rico and the Virgin Islands as the general manager, and ran the company's entire Illinois operation. Bill progressively rose through the ranks to become, at 36, the company's youngest corporate officer and division president.

"I was with Xerox for 17 years. I look at the company as my family. Now, I look at SAP as my family. I think you have only a few career moves in your life where you can say the company is your family, and that's a blessing. Most people can't say that even once.

"Do I have dreams and aspirations? Absolutely. Are they tied to a particular corner office or a particular role here or elsewhere? No. The future is so exciting when you don't try to figure it all out, when you leave a little flexibility. I might have new interests two or three years from now that I can't even conceive of today. Why would I lock myself in any box?

"I honestly believe that the best way to get your dreams fulfilled in life is to help the people who count on you to achieve theirs. And if I do that well, everything is going to take care of itself, one way or another."

A FINAL WORD

We live in a time of great skepticism about leadership in general and business leaders in particular. The media give us plenty to complain about with stories about corporate greed and irresponsibility. But do we want to swallow this information whole, like so much fast food, or do we want to challenge these stereotypes and come to our own conclusions?

By sitting down with these leaders, I saw beyond the stereotypes and in the process received a mini-MBA. I was struck by the calmness, humility, and openness of each CEO. Despite difficult business challenges (and, in many cases, equally challenging personal obstacles), they radiated positive, optimistic attitudes.

After my interviews, I confirmed my own beliefs—that most CEOs are honest, down to earth, and caring people. They value their organizations and employees and are far from being arrogant or reckless. They view themselves as stewards and protectors of important resources—most importantly, people. I hope that some of your assumptions and beliefs about corporate leaders were at least challenged, if not changed.

I also believe that many of the leadership lessons in this book transcend the business world and can help anyone, regardless of their career or position in life. I challenge you to adopt these lessons to your own life. I encourage you to seek out a mentor in your field or area of interest. You will not only learn a great deal from that person, but about yourself as well. If you have the entrepreneurial itch, scratch it. Figure out the legacy you want to leave behind, for others to enjoy and learn from, and find ways to build it. And, lastly, try to establish and maintain balance in your life, to remember what's most important at the end of the day. Be true to yourself and those who are closest to you.

I wish you peace and prosperity on your journey.

Scott D. Rosen

P.S. I would love to receive feedback or have a conversation with you about any aspect of this book. Feel free to email me at scott.rosen@rosengroup.com or call me at 856-470-1400, ext. 104.

ABOUT THE AUTHOR

Scott D. Rosen is President and CEO of The Rosen Group, Inc. and Transformations Holistic Learning Center, both headquartered in Voorhees, N.J.

Established in 1995, The Rosen Group's mission is to transform the human resources strategy of organizations from broken to fixed, from good to great, and from great to world class. The Rosen Group provides strategic consulting services to align a company's business strategy with its human resource strategy. The Rosen Group also offers human resources staffing at all levels, specializing in HR strategy and management, talent acquisition, compensation, benefits, HRIS, training and development, and employee relations on a contract, direct hire, and contract-to-direct hire basis.

During the past 15 years, Scott has grown The Rosen Group to $10 million in revenue with a staff of over 100 employees. In 2000, The Rosen Group was ranked 146th on the Inc. 500 list of fastest-growing privately-held companies, with growth of 1,790% from 1995-2000.

In 2007, Scott established Transformations Holistic Learning Center specializing in individual and corporate wellness programs. The vision of Transformations is to help individuals, families, and communities realize their highest potential, while contributing to the greater good.

Earlier in his career, Scott served eight years at the General Electric Capital Corporation as a Human Resources Management Expert, and eight years as a Corporate Operations Executive at the CIGNA and Prudential Insurance Companies, specializing in operational efficiency and turn-around efforts.

Scott lives in Cherry Hill, N.J., with his wife Risa and twin children, Cassidy and Lee.

ABOUT THE ROSEN GROUP

The Rosen Group's mission is to transform the human resources strategy of organizations from broken to fixed, from good to great, and from great to world class. Fifteen years after being founded, The Rosen Group stands by its original core values of bottom line results, customer service, continuous improvement, respect, compassion, honesty, courage, and humility.

The Rosen Group provides strategic consulting services. We work with CEOs and HR executives to align their company's business strategy with its human resource strategy. Our services consistently demonstrate that effective human resource strategy has a measurable and significantly positive impact on the top and bottom lines of our clients.

Through Human Resource Strategy Assessments, we determine a company's strengths and the areas in need of significant improvement. Then, our consultants can work with the company on areas such as human resource department organization and design, executive education and coaching, succession planning, executive reward strategies, executive retreats, strategic business planning, executive search, interim executive placement, and executive assessments.

The Rosen Group also offers human resources staffing at all levels, specializing in HR strategy and management, talent acquisition, compensation, benefits, HRIS, training and development, and employee relations. We place employees on a contract, direct hire, and contract-to-direct hire basis.

The Rosen Group is also the premier sponsor of the Human Resources Department of the Year Awards, a distinctive event that brings well-deserved attention to the HR industry as a business and financial partner to organizations. Scott Rosen is the founder of this program.

The Rosen Group
2301 Evesham Road Suite 111
Voorhees, NJ 08043
www.rosengroup.com
856-470-1400

ABOUT TRANSFORMATIONS

Transformations is the Greater Delaware Valley's premier holistic learning center. Its vision is to help individuals, families, and communities realize their highest potential, while contributing to the greater good.

Based in Voorhees, N.J., the company provides professional coaching services and workshops for individuals and organizations seeking balance and integration in every aspect of their lives—physically, emotionally, intellectually, and spiritually.

We believe there are multiple pathways to holistic growth and our services are tailored to best meet the needs of our clients. People need different types of support and knowledge at various stages of their life journey, and Transformations has both the structure and the flexibility to provide these services. We focus on the positive, the possible, and the genius in each of us.

At Transformations, participants can focus on one or more areas of their lives, such as inner peace, relationships, spirituality, career, or finances. We offer both individual coaching and group workshops to help people optimize their choices and gain greater balance.

The Transformations faculty is comprised of entrepreneurs, psychiatrists, business and life coaches, and spiritual leaders. These highly professional and holistically developed individuals possess a diverse body of knowledge to help people achieve their goals. Over the past few years, Transformations has hosted nationally known holistic teachers such as Deepak Chopra, Marianne Williamson, Caroline Myss, Jack Canfield, Harville Hendrix, John Holland, and Debbie Ford.

Transformations Holistic Learning Center
2301 Evesham Road, Suite 109
Voorhees, NJ 08043
www.readytotransform.com
856-470-1399

THE CEOS AND THEIR COMPANIES

Joel Adams
President
Devon Consulting
950 West Valley Rd., Suite 2607, Wayne, PA 19087
(610) 964-5703
www.devonconsulting.com

Founded in 1982, Devon Consulting was one of the pioneers in professional IT staffing in the Philadelphia area. Throughout the 1980s and 1990s, Devon grew rapidly to become one of the Philadelphia area's leading IT staffing companies.

David J. Adelman
President and CEO
Campus Apartments, Inc
4043 Walnut St., Philadelphia, PA 19104-3513
(215) 243-7000
www.campusapts.com

Campus Apartments, LLC, the oldest and one of the largest privately held student housing companies in the nation, is a leader in the development and management of university affiliated housing. The company has more than $1 billion worth of assets under management with more than 26,000 beds in 23 states.

For nearly 50 years, Campus Apartments has been a pioneer in developing communities and providing turnkey solutions for colleges, universities and institutions.

Timothy M. Andrews
President and CEO
Advertising Specialty Institute
4800 Street Rd., Trevose, PA 19053-6646
(800) 546-1350
www.asicentral.com

The Advertising Specialty Institute is the largest media and marketing organization serving the advertising specialty industry, with a membership of over 26,000 distributor firms (sellers) and supplier firms (manufacturers) of advertising specialties. Supplier firms use ASI print and electronic resources to market products to over 22,000 ASI distributor firms. Distributor firms use ASI print and electronic resources, which contain nearly every product in the industry from more than 3,500 reputable suppliers, to locate supplier firms and to market services to buyers. ASI provides catalogs, information directories, newsletters, magazines, websites, and databases, and offers e-commerce, marketing, and selling tools.

Mary Stengel Austen

President and CEO
Tierney Group
200 South Broad St., 10th Floor, Philadelphia, PA 19102
(215) 790-4100
www.hellotierney.com

Headquartered in Philadelphia, Tierney is a full-service strategic communications agency offering integrated advertising, PR, media and digital solutions. A member of the Interpublic Group of Companies (NYSE: IPG), Tierney also maintains a Harrisburg, PA office, and represents clients including TD Bank, Bayer Environmental Science, IBM, Independence Blue Cross, Fox Chase Cancer Center, McDonald's, PECO, Sun Life Financial, Sunoco, Verizon Wireless, and 6ABC. An agency that traces its roots back to 1942, Tierney is known for high-profile campaigns, media buying prowess, and stand-out creativity in campaigns such as: "Philadelphia, the City That Loves You Back."

Mark Baiada

President and Founder
Bayada Nurses
290 Chester Ave, Moorestown, NJ 08057
(856) 231-1000
www.bayada.com

Founded in 1975, Bayada Nurses has a special purpose—to help people have a safe home life with comfort, independence, and dignity. They provide nursing, rehabilitative, therapeutic, and personal care services to children, adults, and seniors in the comfort of their own homes. They employ over 13,000 nurses, home health aides, and therapists working from more than 170 offices in 18 states and the UK. Our goal at Bayada Nurses is to provide the highest quality home health care services available with compassion, excellence, and reliability—their core values.

Michael Barry
Chairman, Chief Executive Officer, and President
Quaker Chemical Corporation
One Quaker Park, 901 East Hector St., Conshohocken, PA 19428-0809
(610) 832-4000
www.quakerchem.com

Quaker Chemical Corporation is a leading global provider of process chemicals, chemical specialties, services, and technical expertise to a wide range of industries—including steel, automotive, mining, aerospace, tube and pipe, coatings, and construction materials. Their products, technical solutions, and chemical management services enhance their customers' processes, improve their product quality, and lower their costs.

David Binswanger
President and CEO
Binswanger
Two Logan Square, Philadelphia, PA 19103
(215) 448-6000
www.binswanger.com

David Binswanger is president of Binswanger Companies, which advises corporate clients on real estate asset management, investment, sales and leasing, site selection, and property management. The company also provides appraisal and development consulting services.

Peter J. Boni
President and CEO
Safeguard Scientifics, Inc.
435 Devon Park Drive, Building 800, Wayne, PA 19087-1945
(610) 975-4903
www.safeguard.com, Blog: blog.safeguard.com

Founded in 1953 and based in Wayne, PA, Safeguard Scientifics, Inc. (NYSE: SFE) provides growth capital for entrepreneurial and innovative life sciences and technology companies. Safeguard targets life sciences companies in Molecular and Point-of-Care Diagnostics, Medical Devices, Regenerative Medicine and Specialty Pharmaceuticals, and technology companies in Internet/New Media, Financial Services IT, and Healthcare IT with capital requirements of up to $25 million. Safeguard participates in expansion financings, corporate spin-outs, management buyouts, recapitalizations, industry consolidations, and early-stage financings.

Marc Brownstein

President and CEO
Brownstein Group
215 South Broad St., Philadelphia, PA 19107
(215) 735-3470
www.brownsteingroup.com

Brownstein Group is a digitally-centered advertising agency that creates unique brand identities. They execute via digital and traditional advertising, brand strategy, and public relations/social media. The agency was created in 1964 by Berny Brownstein during the creative revolution, and is now led by his son Marc. The agency believes it is important to evolve and stay relevant to anticipate and meet the needs of its clients, which has been key to its success for 46 years. Clients include IKEA, Microsoft, Comcast, and W.L. Gore.

Robert J. Ciaruffoli, CPA

CEO
ParenteBeard LLC
One Liberty Place
1650 Market St, Suite 4500, Philadelphia, PA 19103
(215) 972-2349
www.ParenteBeard.com

ParenteBeard LLC is the mid-Atlantic's leading certified public accounting and consulting firm, with over 1,200 employees serving middle market and small business clients across the region. The 170-partner firm has 26 offices located in Pennsylvania, New Jersey, New York, Maryland, Delaware, and

Texas. The firm is ranked among the Top 20 firms in the U.S. and is an independent member of Baker Tilly International.

Les Cohen
Executive Director
Katz Jewish Community Center of Southern New Jersey
1301 Springdale Rd., Cherry Hill, NJ 08003
(856) 424-4444
www.katzjcc.org

The Katz Jewish Community Center is a vibrant, state of the art facility that provides vital life enhancing programs and services for individuals of all ages and abilities, from infants to the frail elderly to individuals with special needs. The Katz JCC has been in existence for over 70 years and serves people in Camden, Burlington, and Gloucester Counties. Over 20,000 people receive services and participate in a variety of activates at the Center each year.

Cristóbal Conde
President and CEO
SunGard
340 Madison Ave., 7th Floor, New York, NY 10173
(646) 445-1018
www.sungard.com

With revenues of about $5.6 billion in 2008, SunGard is one of the world's leading software and IT services companies, providing software and processing solutions for financial services, higher education and the public sector. SunGard also provides disaster recovery services, managed IT services, information availability consulting services and business continuity management software. It serves over 25,000 customers in more than 70 countries. Headquartered in Wayne, Pa., SunGard has 20,000 employees worldwide, with about 2,000 based in the Philadelphia area.

Joseph Coradino
President
PREIT
200 South Broad St., 3rd Floor, Philadelphia, PA 19102
(215) 875-0746
www.preit.com

Pennsylvania Real Estate Investment Trust (PREIT), celebrating its 50th Anniversary in 2010, is one of the first equity REITs in the U.S. With 54 retail properties including 38 shopping malls, 13 community centers, and three properties under development, the Philadelphia-headquartered company has a primary investment focus on retail shopping malls and community centers. The company's entrepreneurial spirit, innovative property redevelopment and leasing strategies, and commitment to providing quality shopping experiences translates into value for retailers, clients, shareholders, and shoppers. PREIT's diversified portfolio consists of properties across the eastern half of the United States, primarily in the mid-Atlantic region.

Don Correll
President and CEO
American Water
1025 Laurel Oak Rd., Voorhees, NJ 08043
(856) 346-8203
www.amwater.com

Founded in 1886, American Water is the largest investor-owned U.S. water and wastewater utility company. With headquarters in Voorhees, N.J., the company employs approximately 7,300 dedicated professionals who provide drinking water, wastewater, and other related services to approximately 15 million people in 32 states and Ontario, Canada.

Harold T. Epps
President and CEO
PRWT Services, Inc.
1835 Market St., Suite 800, Philadelphia, PA 19103
(215) 569-8810
www.prwt.com

PRWT Services, Inc. (PRWT) is a nationally recognized, diversified enterprise consisting of pharmaceutical manufacturing and value added services, facilities management, and business process solutions services. PRWT, one of the largest minority-owned businesses headquartered in the Greater Philadelphia Region, has been ranked in the top 100 minority-owned businesses in America by *Black Enterprise* magazine for nine consecutive years (ranked #25 in 2009 and named Industrial/Service Company of the Year). Since 1988, PRWT has continually expanded its business process solutions operations and added facilities management services and active pharmaceutical ingredients (APIs) manufacturing through its U.S. Facilities, Inc. and Cherokee Pharmaceuticals LLC subsidiaries.

Joseph Frick
President and CEO
Independence Blue Cross
1901 Market St., Philadelphia, PA 19103
(215) 241-2006
www.ibx.com

Independence Blue Cross is a leading health insurer in southeastern Pennsylvania. Nationwide, Independence Blue Cross and its affiliates provide coverage to nearly 3.3 million people. For more than 70 years, Independence Blue Cross has offered high-quality health care coverage tailored to meet the changing needs of members, employers, and health care professionals. Independence Blue Cross's HMO and PPO health care plans have consistently received the highest ratings from the National Committee for Quality Assurance. Independence Blue Cross is an independent licensee of the Blue Cross and Blue Shield Association.

Dr. Jeffrey Graves
CEO
C&D Technologies
1400 Union Meeting Rd., Blue Bell, PA 19422-0858
(215) 619-2700
www.cdtechno.com

Based in Blue Bell, Pa., C&D Technologies is a 100-year-old company that produces and markets electrical power storage and conversion products, including industrial batteries, high frequency switching power supplies, and converters. These products provide reliable backup power for critical infrastructure, such as telecommunication systems, data centers, computer rooms, bank and financial systems, and many other applications.

David Griffith

President and CEO
Modern Group Ltd.
2501 Durham Rd., Bristol, PA 19007-6903
(215) 943-9100
www.moderngroup.com

Modern Group Ltd. is a holding company based in Bristol, Pa. One of the nation's largest industrial distributors, Modern has interests in the material handling, industrial distribution and services, power generation, construction, rental, and municipal industries. Modern employs 650 people and does business in 22 locations in four states. Modern represents such lines as Hyster, Generac, New Holland, JLG, Genie, Western, and Swenson. They provide sales, service, parts, and rentals across our product line. Their staff excels at application design, engineering, and problem solving.

Jane Golden Heriza

Executive Director
Mural Arts Program
Lincoln Financial Mural Arts Center at the Thomas Eakins House,
1727-29 Mt. Vernon St., Philadelphia, PA 19130
(215) 685-0760
www.muralarts.org

The Mural Arts Program is the nation's largest mural program. Since 1984, Mural Arts has created over 3,000 murals and works of public art, earning Philadelphia international recognition as the "City of Murals." Mural Arts engages over 100 communities each year in the transformation of neighborhoods through the mural-making process, while award-winning, free art education programs serve nearly 2,000 youth at sites throughout the city and at-risk teens through education outreach programs. Mural Arts also serves adult offenders in local prisons and rehabilitation centers, using the restorative power of art to break the cycle of crime and violence in our communities. Each year, nearly 10,000 residents and visitors tour the program's outdoor art gallery, which has become part of Philadelphia's civic landscape and a source of pride and inspiration.

Kevin S. Kan
President and CEO
American Auto Wash, Inc.
512 East King Rd., Malvern PA 19355
(610) 296-4126 ext. 311
www.griffinpetrol.com

Gentle Touch Car Wash, along with Griffin Petroleum, is wholly owned by American Auto Wash, Inc., a company incorporated in the State of Pennsylvania in 1969. Currently American Auto Wash owns and operates over 18 retail gasoline stations and 20 full service and exterior car washes under the Gentle Touch Car Wash brand, employing over 300 people. Gentle Touch Car Wash is one of the nation's largest independently owned car wash chains.

Rudy Karsan
CEO
Kenexa
650 E. Swedesford Rd., Wayne, PA 19087
(610) 971-6101
www.kenexa.com

Kenexa® provides business solutions for human resources. They help global organizations multiply business success by identifying the best individuals for every job and fostering optimal work environments for every organization. For more than 20 years, Kenexa has studied human behavior and team dynamics in the workplace, and has developed the software solutions, business processes, and expert consulting that help organizations impact positive business outcomes through HR. Kenexa is the only company that offers a comprehensive suite of unified products and services that support the entire employee lifecycle from pre-hire to exit.

Rick A. Lepley
Former CEO
A.C. Moore
www.acmoore.com
130 A C Moore Dr., Berlin, NJ 08009
(856) 768-4930

A.C. Moore is a specialty retailer offering a vast selection of arts, crafts, and floral merchandise to a broad demographic of customers. The first A.C. Moore store opened in Moorestown, New Jersey in 1985. Today there are 135 stores located in the eastern U.S., from Maine to Florida. The company is devoted to being a customer's first choice for product selection, value, and service, to inspire and fulfill unlimited creative possibilities. The A. C. Moore assortment of merchandise consists of more than 60,000 stock keeping units, or SKUs, with approximately 40,000 SKUs offered at each store at any one time. The company also offers custom framing in each location. In-store events and programs for children and adults provide hands-on arts and crafts experience and encourage the creativity of customers.

Daniel L. Lombardo
CEO
Volunteers of America Delaware Valley, Inc.
235 White Horse Pike, West Collingswood, NJ 08107
(856) 854-4660
www.voadv.org

Volunteers of America Delaware Valley is the greater Philadelphia regional affiliate of Volunteers of America, a national, faith-based nonprofit founded in 1896. Volunteers of America Delaware Valley is a professional human services organization that annually serves more than 11,000 men, women, and children in New Jersey, Pennsylvania, and Delaware. They shelter homeless people and help them find permanent housing. Volunteers of America helps people struggling with behavioral health issues or development disabilities. And they also help ex-offenders re-enter their communities, reconcile with their families, and resume their working lives.

Bill McDermott
Co-CEO, Member SAP Executive Board
SAP AG
3999 West Chester Pike, Newtown Square, PA 19073
(610) 661-1000
www.sap.com

SAP is the world's leading provider of business software, offering applications and services that enable companies of all sizes and in more than 25 industries to become best-run businesses. With more than 95,000 customers in over 120 countries, the company is listed on several exchanges, including the Frankfurt stock exchange and NYSE, under the symbol SAP. For more information, visit www.sap.com.

Jill Michal

President and CEO
United Way of Southeastern Pennsylvania
1709 Benjamin Franklin Parkway, Philadelphia, PA 19103
(215) 665-2530
www.liveunitedsepa.org

United Way of Southeastern Pennsylvania is part of a national network of more than 1,300 locally governed organizations that work to create lasting positive changes in communities and in people's lives. United Way engages the community to identify the underlying causes of the most significant local issues, develops strategies, and pulls together financial and human resources to address them and measure the results. United Way is advancing the common good in southeastern Pennsylvania by focusing on education for children, income for families, and health for seniors.

Richard P. Miller

President and CEO
Virtua
401 Rte. 73 N., 50 Lake Center Dr. Ste. 401, Marlton, NJ 08053
(856) 355-0005
www.virtua.org

As the largest comprehensive healthcare provider in southern New Jersey, Virtua delivers an outstanding patient experience through Programs of Excellence in women's health, pediatrics, cancer, cardiology, orthopedics, neuroscience, surgery, and wellness. Virtua opened a new Health and Wellness Center in 2009 and will open a $463 million digital replacement hospital in 2011. Virtua's Berlin, Marlton, Mount Holly, and Voorhees hospitals and Camden outpatient center continue to expand technology and services. Virtua employs 8,400 personnel and 1,800 physicians as medical staff. Virtua created partnerships and alliances with organizations, including GE, Fox Chase Cancer Center, Nemours A. I. DuPont Hospital for Children, and the Philadelphia Flyers. Virtua is consistently acknowledged for quality and service. It has adopted process improvement tools, including Six Sigma and Lean, and is ranked a #1 Best Place to Work, regionally and nationally.

Mike Pearson

President
Contemporary Staffing Solutions, Inc.
161 Gaither Drive, Suite 100, Mount Laurel, NJ 08054
(856) 222-0020
www.contemporarystaffing.com

Award-winning Contemporary Staffing Solutions, Inc. is a prominent leader in the staffing industry throughout the Delaware Valley. Named to the Philadelphia 100 and to SJ Top 25 Fastest Growing Privately Held Companies, CSS hosts three successful divisions: Administrative and Office Support, CSS Technical Services, and CSS Professional Search. CSS places professional candidates in various direct hire, temp-to-hire, temporary, and contract positions.

Ted Peters

Chairman and CEO
Bryn Mawr Trust Company
801 Lancaster Ave., Bryn Mawr, PA 19010
(610) 581-4800
www.bmtc.com

The Bryn Mawr Trust Company has been a trusted advisor to families, individuals and businesses since 1889. Based on a tradition of unparalleled customer service, their mission is to provide the highest quality service, expertise and support to their clients. They are truly dedicated to making a positive contribution in the community they serve. The Bryn Mawr Trust Company is a wholly owned subsidiary of Bryn Mawr Bank Corporation, which also owns The Bryn Mawr Trust Company of Delaware and Lau Associates LLC. Lau Associates LLC represents sophisticated solutions to the specialized financial service needs of our clients. Bryn Mawr Bank Corporation stock is publicly held and traded on NASDAQ Global Market under the symbol of BMTC. Bryn Mawr Trust offers a full range of personal and business banking services, consumer and commercial loans, equipment leasing, mortgages, insurance, and wealth management services, including investment management, trust and estate administration, retirement planning, custody services, brokerage, and tax planning and preparation. Their professionals are acknowledged leaders in their fields. They work together as a dedicated team to bring the highest level of expertise, integrity and objective advice to our clients. The Bryn Mawr Trust Company serves clients across the country and has deep roots in the Philadelphia area, with a combination of full-service offices on the Main Line and Chester County, and other service offices in seven select retirement communities.

Irvin E. Richter

Chairman and CEO
Hill International, Inc.
303 Lippincott Centre, Marlton, NJ 08053
(856) 810-6200
www.hillintl.com

Hill International (NYSE:HILL) is a worldwide construction consulting firm, employing over 2300 professionals in 80 global offices, offering project management and construction claims consulting services to both public and private clients. Having participated in over 5,000 project assignments with a total construction value of over $250 billion, Hill has managed all phases of the construction process. From pre-design through completion, Hill has experience in all facets of project management. *Engineering News-Record* magazine recently ranked Hill as the 8th largest construction management firm in the U.S. The Project Management Group is complemented by a world renowned Construction Claims Group, which has participated in over 25,000 disputes valued in excess of $100 billion.

Ed Snider

Chairman
Comcast-Spectacor
3601 South Broad St., Philadelphia, PA 19148
(215) 952-5211
www.comcast-spectacor.com

Comcast-Spectacor is the Philadelphia-based sports and entertainment company which owns the Philadelphia Flyers (NHL), the Philadelphia 76ers (NBA), two Philadelphia arenas, the Wachovia Center and Wachovia

Spectrum, four Flyers Skate Zone community ice skating and hockey rinks, and Comcast SportsNet Philadelphia. In addition, Comcast-Spectacor is also the principal owner of Global Spectrum, the fastest growing firm in the public assembly management field, with more than 80 facilities throughout the U.S. and Canada; Ovations Food Services, a food and beverage service provider; New Era Tickets, a ticketing and marketing company for public assembly facilities; Front Row Marketing Services, a commercial rights sales company; and 3601 Creative Group, a full-service in-house advertising agency. In a partnership with Disson Skating, Comcast-Spectacor annually produces 10 nationally televised figure skating spectaculars on NBC.

Robert Soper

President and CEO
Mohegan Sun at Pocono Downs
1280 Highway 315, Wilkes-Barre, PA 18702-7002
(570) 831-2101
www.poconodowns.com

With 55,000 square feet of gaming space holding 2,500 slot and electronic virtual table games, Mohegan Sun at Pocono Downs offers countless opportunities for gaming fun and success. While the location is unrivaled for gaming services and amenities, they've also brought in a variety of dining options that people in this area are craving. Whether it's fine dining at Ruth's Chris Steak House or Rustic Kitchen Bistro and Bar, casual dining at Timber's Buffet, or a delicious quick meal at the Sky Food Court, there's something to satisfy every appetite. Shopping is a whole new experience. And they've put the "life" in nightlife with the fabulous Sunburst Bar in the heart of the action, and eclectic entertainment and high kickin' fun at Breaker's Bar. There's so much to do and see here that you really do need to experience it for yourself. And while it may be impossible to do it all in one day, it's the kind of place you'll want to return to time and again.

Jay Spector

CEO
JEVS Human Services
1845 Walnut St., Philadelphia, PA 19103
(215) 854-1804
www.jevshumanservices.org

JEVS Human Services enhances the employability, independence, and quality of life of individuals through a broad range of programs. Founded in 1941 by 25 Jewish concerned citizens, Jewish Employment and Vocational Service was established to help Jewish refugees adjust to life in Philadelphia. Today, JEVS Human Services is one of the largest, private nonprofit organizations in the Delaware Valley. JEVS Human Services and its support staff of nearly 1,000 employees run more than 20 successful programs that provide skills development, job readiness and career services, vocational rehabilitation, recovery services, adult and residential day services, and in-home personal assistance.

Howard B. Stoeckel

President and CEO
Wawa, Inc.
260 W. Baltimore Pike, Red Roof, Wawa, PA 19063
(610) 358-8046
www.wawa.com

Wawa, Inc., a privately held company, began in 1803 as an iron foundry in New Jersey. Toward the end of the 19th Century, owner George Wood took an interest in dairy farming and the family began a small processing plant in Wawa, Pa., in 1902. The milk business was a huge success, due to its quality, cleanliness, and "certified" process. As home delivery of milk declined in the early 1960's, Grahame Wood, George's grandson, opened the first Wawa Food Market in 1964 as an outlet for dairy products. Today, Wawa operates more than 570 stores in Pennsylvania, New Jersey, Delaware, Maryland, and Virginia. All Wawa stores offer a large fresh food service selection under the Wawa brand, including built-to-order hoagies, freshly-brewed coffee, quality dairy products, hot breakfast sandwiches, wraps, bakery products, and fruits.

Dave Yost

President and CEO
AmerisourceBergen
1300 Morris Dr., Suite 100, Chesterbrook, PA 19087-5594
(610) 727-7170
www.amerisourcebergen.com

AmerisourceBergen is one of the world's largest pharmaceutical services companies serving the U.S., Canada, and selected global markets. Servicing both pharmaceutical manufacturers and healthcare providers in the pharmaceutical supply channel, the company provides drug distribution and related services designed to reduce costs and improve patient outcomes. AmerisourceBergen's service solutions range from pharmacy automation and pharmaceutical packaging, to reimbursement and pharmaceutical consulting services. With more than $71 billion in annual revenue, AmerisourceBergen is headquartered in Valley Forge, Pa., and employs approximately 10,000 people. AmerisourceBergen is ranked #26 on the Fortune 500 list.

Joseph S. Zuritsky
Chairman and CEO
Parkway Corporation
150 North Broad St., Philadelphia, PA 19102
(215) 575-4001
www.parkwaycorp.com

Parkway Corporation is Philadelphia's premier parking and real estate development company. For three generations, this family-run business has developed over $250 million of real estate in the U.S. and Canada, consisting of parking garages, surface parking lots, office buildings, retail spaces, and condominiums. The current portfolio consists of owned locations, strategic managed accounts containing thousands of parking spaces, and hundreds of thousands of square feet of restaurant, retail, and office space. Parkway presently employs over 600 people and has operations in seven markets in the U.S. and Canada.

Breinigsville, PA USA
29 September 2010
246294BV00001B/2/P

9 781452 035130